Applause

My grandfather, Mahatma Gandhi, believed as long as we live in fear we will never be truly free. We are afraid of change because we are afraid of insecurity. Yet change is the only way we will save humanity from certain disaster. The Change Code *will help you understand why change is necessary and how to achieve it. An excellent read.*

~**ARUN GANDHI**, Founder, M.K.Gandhi Institute of Nonviolence, Rochester, NY, and author of *The Gift of Anger* a best-seller translated into 30 languages.

"In a time of distraction and disconnection, The Change Code *offers hope and direction. Monica Bourgeau has compiled a brilliant body of work that addresses challenges on every level-- from the discontent individual to the struggling corporation, and certainly employs strategies that can be applied on a global scale. Well written and smartly executed, I highly recommend everyone read this wise and timely book!"*

~**TAMARA DORRIS**, MA author of *Imagine That!* and *Mind Over Matter*

"The perspective that this book shares is critical to the successful navigation of a very uncertain future. Read it and take responsibility!"

~**PETER MERRY**, Ph.D. Chief Innovation Officer at Ubiquity University and Founder, Center for Human Emergence NL

"Monica's work is a refreshing reminder of the power of human creativity. This book, and the associated materials, adds a valuable contribution to the Gravesian lineage. Use this work to reveal and work with the deeper codes of humanness as together we make the trapeze-like leap towards a new era".

~**CHRISTOPHER COOKE**, MSC Co-founder of 3LM and 5 Deep Limited

"The Change Code *provides a unique look into Humanity's Master Code. It provides a practical application for Graves' theory in reducing polarization and managing today's complex and turbulent times.*"

~**DON EDWARD BECK,** Ph.D., Author of *Spiral Dynamics: Mastering Values, Leadership and Change*; and *Spiral Dynamics in Action*

"BRAVO! I've continued to reflect upon this insightful work, which means this book is effective. I found myself thinking about my personal and professional experiences going through these colors. This book is a helpful guide for any Change Agent looking to better understand and communicate with individuals representing different colors. Watch for the gems of wisdom woven throughout."

~**KAMI NORLAND,** MA, ATR CEO, Integrative Re-Sources

The Change Code

A Practical Guide to
Making a Difference in a Polarized World

by Monica Bourgeau
Foreword by Futurist Steve McDonald

THE CHANGE CODE: A PRACTICAL GUIDE
TO MAKING A DIFFERENCE IN A POLARIZED WORLD

© 2019 by Monica Bourgeau
Published by New Phase Publishing

For information, contact:
New Phase Publishing
www.NewPhasePublishing.com
13203 SE 172nd Ave., Suite 166 #100,
Happy Valley, OR 97086

The author has endeavored to recount facts as accurately as possible.
Published in the United States of America

Paperback ISBN: 978-1-7340655-0-3
Hardcover ISBN: 978-1-7340655-1-0
E-book ISBN: 978-1-7340655-1-0
Library of Congress Control Number: 2019919225

Design and layout by: Jamie Tipton, Open Heart Designs, www.openheartdesigns.com

To my brilliant and supportive husband,
Dave for inspiring me every day.

And to my friend and mentor, Dr. Don Beck
for sharing Graves' amazing work with the world.

Contents

Foreword

Melbourne, Australia is famous for its cultural diversity and excellent coffee, a perfect blend for long conversations with interesting people. I moved there in 2003 and during one of those long conversations, a jovial Scotsman named Ron Laurie introduced me to the work of Dr. Clare W. Graves. Ron and I both worked in organizational development and shared a deep interest in human nature and the mysteries of life. At his suggestion, I picked up a book called *Spiral Dynamics: Mastering Values, Leadership and Change* that explained human development according to Graves' extensive research. Reading that book changed my life.

As fate would have it, Graves passed away in 1986 before releasing his full research findings. The Spiral Dynamics book was published ten years later by Dr. Don Beck and Christopher Cowan, as a novice's guide for the corporate leadership market. Both Beck and Cowan had worked closely with Graves, Beck from soon after meeting him in 1975 and Cowan from 1981. It was many years later though, before his entire work on human biopsychosocial systems and their development became publicly available. The book Graves had been working on, *The Never Ending Quest* was finally published by Cowan and Todorovic in 2005. Graves was a man well ahead of his time and as is often the case, the world needed to catch up before his work could be appreciated.

In 2003, I was on the verge of a breakdown from posttraumatic stress, the result of my war service in Africa and subsequent work as a civilian rescue helicopter pilot. As I navigated that breakdown and breakthrough, somehow I made sense of it with Graves' map of transformational change.

In the midst of it all, his work helped me see this was a process rather than a dead end, which made a huge difference. After time in the hospital and seven months off work I slowly got back on my feet, with a completely new perspective on life—just as his model predicted. That was some validation process!

I was seeing the world through new eyes and had found an "operator's manual" for the human experience.

I had the pleasure of meeting Graves' student and colleague Don Beck and attending a basic Spiral Dynamics Integral (SDi) training course he ran on the Gold Coast in 2005. The following year I flew to Beck's home state of Texas for the annual SDi conference and some further training. My instructor there was Christopher Cooke, a highly experienced British change professional, who'd trained people alongside Beck for a decade. Thanks to support from both Beck and Cooke, in 2008 I hosted a train-the-trainer course at my office in Melbourne and then began teaching SDi in the corporate sector.

According to Graves, human development follows an emergent, cyclical pattern of change through sequential value systems, arising from the interaction between our life conditions and the adaptive nature of our consciousness. As our environmental challenges become more complex, our consciousness adapts and our coping capacity expands accordingly. History shows the evolution of our species has followed this same pattern, driven by increasing complexity. Given our present-day challenges, this is a very reassuring message.

Back in 1974 Clare Graves published an article in *The Futurist* magazine titled "Human Nature Prepares for a Momentous Leap." In it, he introduced his model and described an unprecedented leap forward in human coping capacity, exhibited by a small percentage of his research subjects. These few people displayed extraordinary capacities, placing them well ahead of their peers and mainstream society at the time.

Graves said these subjects:

> ...*solved problems not only more rapidly but they also found more answers than all the others added together. Relative to the others, the rapidity with which (these) subjects could change their point of reference was almost unbelievable.*

These pathfinders were living examples of the values, ethics and extraordinary coping capacity of a future society, almost as if they'd travelled back in time to visit us. I found this predictive aspect of his model both fascinating and tremendously exciting. It's what led me to become a futurist.

Presently our scientific-industrial way of living, the fifth layer of human existence in Graves' model, is clearly in decline. Increasingly challenged by the complexity of a hyperconnected world in flux, our political, economic and other systems are no longer coping. Rather than solving problems like they used to, they're creating new problems, including the polarization of society and the spread of civil unrest. These are symptoms of evolutionary tension. Like a rubber band being pulled backwards on a slingshot, this tension is nature's way of energizing us for our momentous leap forward.

What's missing for most people is a basic understanding of how this non-linear change process works and what it means for our future. Thankfully, that knowledge is right here in your hands.

When Monica Bourgeau reached out to me in early 2019 I was delighted to learn about the book she was writing and grateful for the opportunity to make a small contribution. For the first time ever, we have real-time visibility of a global paradigm shift. The revolution of our own consciousness is one vital aspect of this planetary reset. Where previously we've been surprised and swept off our feet by such tsunamis of change, with this knowledge we have the opportunity to read and ride the waves of revolution. There is no better time to learn about The Change Code and put it into practice.

It's my great pleasure to commend this book to you. I trust it will change your life.

Steve McDonald
Futurist and Executive Director, AADII Mesh Foundation
Byron Bay, Australia

Steve McDonald

Steve McDonald is a futurist and the founder of AADII, a nonprofit change agency, and Future Sense, a podcast and radio show that broadcasts from Byron Bay, Australia. His work supports the ongoing evolution of human consciousness and our global transition beyond the scientific-industrial era.

He has a diverse background spanning military service, management consulting across the government, corporate and nonprofit sectors, and piloting military reconnaissance and civilian rescue helicopters. He has been a director of numerous startup organizations, both commercial and non-profit and is currently Executive Director of the charitable Aadii Mesh Foundation, which operates the AADII change agency. He is also co-founder of Psychedelic Research in Science & Medicine.

Steve has been studying and applying Dr. Clare W. Graves' theory of human development as a change agent since 2003. He applies the model as a futurist for making sense of global paradigm shifts and anticipating future challenges.

He has a long-term interest in mysticism and has studied with a western mystery school and also practiced Taoist martial and healing energy arts for over 20 years. In 2018, he founded a Taoist order to progress the merging of science and spirituality into a unified understanding of our multidimensional existence.

Preface

The Change Code provides a unique look into Humanity's Master Code. It provides a practical application for Graves' theory in reducing polarization and managing today's complex and turbulent times.

Graves' work takes on many different expressions:

(1) sacred and spiritual manifestations and models;
(2) traditional secular psychological and behavioral research: patterns, typologies and processes; and
(3) sophisticated scientific and neurological (mind-brain-chemical) analyses.

Further, one can discover practical applications to enhance competitive teams, effective education, and training approaches. Graves' theory can even be used to enhance holistic health care, preventative medicine, and forms of healing. A leading Canadian magazine called the work of Professor Clare Graves the " theory that explains everything."

Rather than single theories of change or single universal one-size-fits-all solutions, the focus of Graves' theory is on natural design, forms, admixtures, and blends to function, fit and flow. It's what the world needs now, and this book, *The Change Code*, brings it to life.

Don Beck, Ph.D., Denton, TX,
Author of Spiral Dynamics: Mastering Values, Leadership and Change; *and* Spiral Dynamics in Action

Introduction

You're a person who's always been able to come up with solutions to make things better. You're known for your big visions, and the energy and perseverance to make them happen.

But you've hit a brick wall. For a few years, you've felt like the world is taking a dramatic turn for the worse. Everything around you seems to be crumbling. There are so many problems—and they are so *complex*. This time, the sky feels like it's *really* falling.

This is a big deal for you. You're generally an optimist who sees opportunity in even the biggest challenges. You've even been called an idealist, a Pollyanna—you're maybe a little *too* excited about life and the future.

So, this polarized, angry world is bringing you to your knees.

Depending on your situation, some issues are more visible than others. For me, one of these is our healthcare system here in America. I've spent most of my career leading change in healthcare. We have caring and dedicated people working in this profession, but there's no denying the system is severely broken. I don't have to tell you what's happening out there; you see it every day. Huge numbers of uninsured. Millions going without basic health care. Hospitals that are struggling, especially in rural communities where hundreds of them have closed their doors. Drug prices so astronomical that a serious injury or illness can bankrupt the patient. People literally dying from preventable causes in one of the richest countries on earth.

Educational, political, religious, and economic institutions no longer deliver the results they always have for the people they are supposed to serve. Tests prove school compliance instead of measuring individual learning and personal strengths. Politicians represent donors instead of citizens, and religions, too often, continue to divide rather than unite.

And you only have to step outside into the wildfire smoke on a 100-degree day to be reminded of the growing crisis of climate change. Floods, droughts, fires, and hurricanes are all on the rise and becoming more and more severe.

Our problems have become too complex for our existing infrastructure. With more than 7.7 billion people on the planet, problems are both local and global at the same time. They require collaboration to solve. Complex problems are often multiplied by their interrelations with other complex problems.

For example, it turns out that climate change, obesity, and undernutrition are interrelated through our modern food system, according to a report in the British medical journal, *The Lancet*. Researchers found that unhealthy, inequitable, and unsustainable agriculture and food production are major contributors to the obesity and undernutrition epidemics, while also contributing to up to one third of global greenhouse gas emissions. This has led to a new term – a "syndemic," which refers to multiple interrelated epidemics happening at the same time.[1]

If you think too much about these national and global problems, or spend too much time reading the news, your shoulders begin to sag from carrying the weight of the world.

You feel angry—and may begin to dislike people in general.

You're left discouraged and often on the verge of tears. You may be tempted to just look away, but you can't. You have to see and feel all of it. But you can't lose yourself in the abyss of pain either. How are you supposed to create positive change in a world that seems to be crumbling at our feet?

And why does everything have to be so polarized? People can't even communicate with each other anymore. You tiptoe around important issues to avoid a heated backlash. Your friends and family have just stopped talking about anything controversial.

Let's step back for a moment and see if we can achieve some

perspective. Listen, you're still a change leader—even in this turbulent time. What's more, I'm here to tell you that there's hope. Real hope.

While things don't always feel easy right now, it's because we are going through a transition in which great innovations are coming. There are seeds of a new way, with people across the globe stepping forward, working together, being lights in the darkness, and creating positive change.

Not long ago, I was paralyzed by my feelings of helplessness and frustration with the world. Then I discovered the work of Dr. Clare W. Graves. I began to understand the power of what I call The Change Code, Dr. Graves' theory of "spiral dynamics" which predicts and deciphers the developmental process of our society. That sounds lofty, but The Change Code not only explains the situation we're in, it also shows a path forward into a future of amazing possibilities.

Graves did his research from the 1950s to the 1970s. His student and colleague Dr. Don Beck went on to apply that research to some of the most challenging problems in the most turbulent places in the world. This included working with Nelson Mandela in South Africa, playing a key role in ending apartheid without a civil war.

When writing this book, I reached out to Beck, who also co-authored several books on Graves' theory. He spent his life furthering the work of Graves and applying the theory to the hottest tension places in the world, including South Africa and the Middle East. Even though he is now in his 80s, Dr. Beck is still actively applying and sharing this work with others, like myself, who feel a deep connection to the theory and the larger purpose of applying it to make the world a better place.

Honestly, it's mind-boggling that we don't hear more about Spiral Dynamics. Graves' discovery has been called "Humanity's Master Code" and the "Theory of Everything." Beck says it's like a "master key" and "[Graves] might well have broken the code to human survival."

There are already books out there, and a growing Integral movement that incorporates Graves' work, but many of the resources can be complex and difficult to follow, one of the many things that prompted me to write this book.

Now that I understand The Change Code, I see it *everywhere*, from patterns in nature to the world's most successful companies such as Whole Foods and Southwest Airlines, to talks by Tony Robbins, and small interactions throughout my day.

The Change Code has captured my mind and my heart, and changed the way I view humanity and the world forever. I hope it will do the same for you. It provides answers to the big questions we are grappling with, as well as a roadmap for moving forward. It's exactly what I needed when I was feeling so helpless – and exactly what we need in our world right now.

The Change Code shows how the world is made up of individuals operating from different layers. These layers are based on people's value systems and the complexity of their lives. Each value system has its own unique paradigm and user manual for societal organization, including its perspectives on politics, religion, and education. As we collectively experience more and more complex conditions, more of us evolve into and incorporate the next layer. In a nutshell, that's what's happening now—we're evolving as a society—even though it doesn't necessarily feel like it.

So, how do you deal with the inevitable conflicts, and stand up as a leader in these challenging times? Differences in value systems cause misunderstanding, polarization, hostility, and even war. We can use The Change Code to more smoothly transition from these feelings of fear, powerlessness, and disconnection into a more self-aware society that understands, accounts for, and even benefits from our differences. A society where everyone belongs.

Just like humanity's transition from a hunter/gatherer to farmer, and again from an agrarian society to an industrial one, we will now inevitably transition into a new era.

But *how* we do it is our choice.

We can stand by while the world falls deeper into a trough of chaos and confusion, hoping things eventually work out. Or, we can actively help society emerge into a higher level of consciousness, with sustainable systems; connected resilient communities; communication and collaboration between every layer; and new coping skills and tools to face the challenges of tomorrow. The future depends on how we choose to respond today.

So, yes, we are in the midst of a transformational shift for humanity, and the amazing thing is—this was totally predictable. Just as every single stage of human and societal development before now has been predictable.

Think about it. Humans have gone through transformational change before: the agricultural revolution, the Renaissance, the industrial revolution. These are all times that we've moved from one very established world view to a completely new one.

And as our life conditions have become more complex, human consciousness has also had to adapt to survive.

Today, we're in the middle of the biggest change ever: We are moving from a very rational, analytical and materialistic era into one that is more humanistic and communal. It's going to take understanding and collaboration. It's going to take leaders who are courageous, humble, and comfortable with uncertainty.

The new paradigm emerging must inevitably lead to new systems. Many of our current systems are crumbling and breaking down. As changemakers and visionaries, you will be the ones who see possible solutions, help us tell new stories, and identify which systems need to be replaced, and how that will happen. You are the pathfinders.

This book is my interpretation of how Graves' theory works, as well as an action plan for change leaders based on this theory. Spoiler alert: Our society isn't crumbling—it's in the midst of a major transformation. Because existing systems aren't adapting quickly enough to keep up with this transformation, the things that no longer work are falling away. And the new systems that will replace them aren't fully developed or in place yet. Plus, we're not even sure yet what those systems should look like.

Understanding the Change Code holds the key not only to the survival of mankind, but to creating a thriving world for all living beings. And we can also use it in our daily lives, our own personal growth, and the way we communicate with each other.

The Change Code gives me hope and optimism for the future, so much so that sharing it with leaders, visionaries, and changemakers like yourself has become my life's work. Because, while I am a diehard idealist, I know we need all hands on deck to make it through the coming decades. Working together, I know we will prevail.

After reading this book, you'll understand the Code, and be better able predict the changes coming down the pike. You'll be able to speak to your audience using their language, and find solutions that heal the world and change the future.

The Change Code incorporates 7 principles that will put you in a position to change the world.

The 7 Principles of The Change Code

1. **Commit to Being an Agent for Change.** Learn the skills and tools to facilitate change: knowing the Change Code value systems (colors), understanding complex systems and polarities, and polarity mapping/management. Practice these skills by taking action and honoring the 7 Principles.

2. **Do your Inner Work First.** Understand your own values and triggers, so that you can better understand the world. Practice extreme self-care to stay grounded and take care of your energy for the long game. You must be able to navigate the complexity and triggers of a polarized world without burning out. Live in alignment with your unique purpose and values.

3. **Encourage Positive Expression of Every Layer of The Change Code.** Agents for Change accept different value systems while designing future institutions, organizations, and opportunities. Encourage the positive expression of each layer as you engineer the future.

4. **Find Common Ground and Understand Who You Are Trying to Help.** Learn ways to communicate with others, and know what they value. Encourage open communication and dialogue that limits polarization and extremism, which is absolutely necessary for finding workable solutions.

5. **Build Resilient Community, Connection, and Opportunities for Communication.** Support individuals and society as a whole, working to reduce polarization, isolation, and loneliness. Gather groups together to work on solutions to complex problems that are a win/win for everyone.

6. **Engage Others in Something Bigger than All of Us.** When facing complex problems like education and homelessness, Agents for Change establish superordinate goals, which are shared by individuals from different groups, and inspire collaboration and cooperation. To create a new future, create and tell a new story.

7. **Develop New Systems to Solve More Complex Problems.** Agents for Change envision, develop, and implement solutions that allow everyone to move into the next phase of human development.

Find a downloadable, printable version of the 7 Principles at www.TheChangeCode.net/Resources.

The world is shifting and changing, but as visionary leaders, we can prepare and guide this evolution to a whole new positive way of being.

The present moment finds our society attempting to negotiate the most difficult, but at the same time the most exciting transition the human race has faced to date. It is not merely a transition to a new

level of existence but the start of a new 'movement' in the symphony of human history.
—*Clare Graves in The Futurist magazine, 1974*

We are living in a phenomenal time. I wrote this book to share the power of The Change Code so you can accelerate transformation in your own corner of the world. And my greatest hope is that you will start to feel excited again about the future and be the change you know you are.

If I share this information in the way that I hope to, I guarantee that, like me, you will never look at the world in the same way again.

CHAPTER 1

Why Can't We Be Friends?

There is too much at stake for us to surrender to the politics of polarization.
~BRAD HENRY

My friend Amy was obviously frustrated and irritated when she sat down for lunch. Her face was red, and she had an unmistakable scowl on her face. She told me she and her husband had a heated discussion before she came to meet with me. I listened to her for a few minutes and then mentioned the title of my book. A look of hope came over her face.

"Well, I can't wait to read it, because we need some help with polarization at my house," she said. "The only thing Ben and I fight about any more is politics, but, boy, do we fight when that topic comes up. We've just had to agree to avoid discussing politics altogether. I hate it. Why do we have this divide?"

Amy's experience isn't unique. I've heard similar stories from many individuals.

Polarization is increasing. People are hurting and being hurt by it. We can all feel it. The extremes have taken hold, and we're losing any common ground we once had. We see this polarization in politics, religion, and education; between classes, races, and family members.

How are we supposed to address humanity's biggest challenges when we can't even have a *conversation*?

In this chapter, we'll discuss the nature of today's problems and our polarized world, what causes polarization, and what we can do to create more unity in both ourselves and in our society.

What is Polarization?

According to the Oxford Dictionary, Polarization is the *"the act of separating or making people separate into two groups with completely opposite opinions."*[2]

Polarity—having opposite extremes—is a naturally occurring phenomenon. Think of light/dark, good/bad, north/south, left/right, introvert/extrovert, up/down, masculine/feminine, yin/yang, the list goes on. We tend to focus on polarities to simplify concepts, overlooking the spaces in between, because it's easier to identify the extremes as a way of understanding how things work. Children, for example, learn start/finish, before they grasp the concepts of halfway done, or three-fourths there.

Natural or not, though, an increased focus on polarity creates an "us vs. them" mentality in human beings. We've got winners vs. losers, right vs. wrong, liberals vs. conservatives, etc. This creates an over-simplified, black and white view of what is in fact a nuanced and complex world, neglecting the many areas of gray. We drift toward the extremes, begin to lose our center, and see the other side as evil. We forget our common ground.

In his book, *Awakening the Global Mind*, Ashok Gangadean calls polarization the result of egocentric thought patterns. When we can see only one right or wrong answer, that is our ego at work. He also refers to a discussion from this place as an "egologue" rather than a dialogue. Even if you are talking to someone else, if you are speaking only through the lens of your own world view and aren't listening with an open heart and an open mind, you are not engaged in dialogue. Does this sound like some of the conversations you've had lately?[3]

Humans have always been polarized—it's a natural phenomenon in the first layers of human development, often tied closely to our survival. However, when we reach the higher levels of consciousness, we understand the value of paradox: when two things that appear to be in opposition are actually both true at the same time. Instead of seeing the world in black and white, we begin to understand that issues are complex. We become more comfortable with shades of gray. For example, around the issue of immigration in the United States, it is possible to be concerned about the increased number of immigrants and enforcement of our existing laws, and to also be concerned about the plight of human beings fleeing war, civil unrest, and corruption. It doesn't have to be one or the other.

There are many situations like that in the world today. Our problems have become more and more complex; in fact, they are downright wicked.

Today's Problems are Wicked

In part, problems have become more challenging because we are living in a time with the most parallel, yet varied, active value systems of any time in human history. What this means is we see examples of people and societies operating in almost every layer of the multi-layered value system. Different value systems mean different (often opposing) views of the world and different views on how problems should be addressed.

Wicked Problems:

- *Ongoing, chronic issues*
- *Unavoidable and unsolvable*
- *No one right solution only "good enough for now" solutions*
- *Solutions vary depending on your values & perspective*
- *Solutions create new problems to address*
- *Require a mindset shift*
- *Requires ongoing collaboration with others*
- *Paradoxical*

In one of those value layers (Orange, which I'll explain later in the book), there are "experts" who can be brought in to present us with clear-cut solutions to many of our problems based on scientific evidence. You see this every night on the news. While this approach may still work for many dilemmas, the increasingly complex problems we face today don't have clear-cut solutions. That's because the solutions to the newer and harder problems involve underlying values and paradoxes. That means that individuals view the problems and solutions differently, depending on their value system. These are the "Wicked Problems," a term coined by design theorist and professor, Horst Rittel.[4]

Wicked Problems are chronic, ongoing issues that are both unsolvable and unavoidable. When you apply customary problem-solving, you only make them worse.

Wicked Problems are part of a complex system, and can't be "solved," only continually navigated. This is a mindset shift for most of us because we love simple, clear solutions. With these more complex problems, however, any "solution" creates new problems and unintended consequences because of the interconnectedness of the system. Consider climate change or healthcare. Facing these problems requires tough choices and sacrifices, mutual understanding, genuine interactions across multiple perspectives, and innovative approaches that also address the tensions between the different value systems.

There are multiple ways to address Wicked Problems, and they vary greatly depending on the group or individual's value system, location, and perspective. For example, trying to address poverty in rural Texas would look very different than it would in rural Kenya. Similarities may exist, but a one-size-fits-all approach would be doomed to failure.

Every Wicked Problem is also a symptom of another problem. For example, reducing the time schoolchildren have to eat lunch to allow for more time at recess may seem like a good idea. However, it could also create a new behavior (and problem) related to nutrition, such as students eating less due to the time constraint, or encouraging them to eat convenience foods that aren't necessarily healthy. Wicked Problems force us to behave differently. The solutions often require us to adapt, and move through a series of temporary solutions.[5]

So how do you know if a problem is Wicked? A wicked problem will also have polarities, and likely multiple polarities. Polarities are seemingly opposing ideas or actions. Both sides of a polarity are interdependent which means when you choose one, you also neglect the other.

Some examples of polarities include:

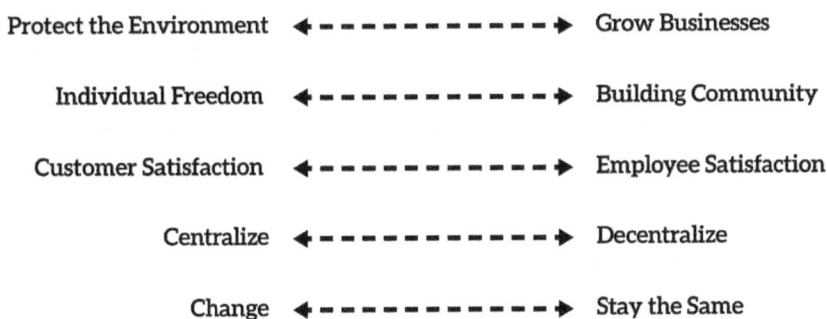

Protect the Environment ◆ ‒ ‒ ‒ ‒ ‒ ‒ ‒ ‒ ‒ ➤ Grow Businesses

Individual Freedom ◆ ‒ ‒ ‒ ‒ ‒ ‒ ‒ ‒ ‒ ➤ Building Community

Customer Satisfaction ◆ ‒ ‒ ‒ ‒ ‒ ‒ ‒ ‒ ‒ ➤ Employee Satisfaction

Centralize ◆ ‒ ‒ ‒ ‒ ‒ ‒ ‒ ‒ ‒ ➤ Decentralize

Change ◆ ‒ ‒ ‒ ‒ ‒ ‒ ‒ ‒ ‒ ➤ Stay the Same

One question you can ask yourself is, "Is this a problem we can solve, or is it an ongoing polarity, paradox, or dilemma that we must manage well?"[6] If it has ongoing polarities, it's a Wicked Problem.

Unfortunately, our current systems weren't designed for this level of complexity. As a result, many people feel their needs and beliefs aren't being represented. Add in the growing distrust of our political system, the news media, the increasing complexity of our problems, so-called "experts," and the process itself, and often the result is an environment ripe for polarization. We see people on the other side as evil, rather than recognizing that it's the problem itself that's wicked. But when we understand the nature of Wicked Problems and the values that underlie them and their solutions, we can stop blaming others and begin working together.

To break this down, let's look at a Wicked Problem more closely.

Consider a populated region with a limited water supply. Everyone needs water: for people and their homes and lawns, for healthy rivers and ecosystems, for recreation, for open space and wildlife habitat, for farms and the local food economy, and for economic vitality in general.

While most people would agree these are all important needs, emotions run high when it comes time to prioritize. And, when you move one lever in one area, the other areas also change. Say for instance, you decided to build a dam to help generate electricity and create a reserve of water for the dry season. This one change affects the migration patterns of fish in the river and the fishing industry; it reduces the water available to a large strawberry farm, increasing the cost of produce, which both affect the local economy. It also causes water shortages in some cities during peak-usage times, increasing the cost of water to residents and requiring restricted hours for watering. It's like pushing over one domino in a long string, sending a jolt throughout the entire line.

There are several polarities in this example, including:

Conserve Water ◀ ▬ ▬ ▬ ▬ ▬ ▬ ▬ ▬ ▶ Irrigate Crops

Protect Wildlife ◀ ▬ ▬ ▬ ▬ ▬ ▬ ▬ ▬ ▶ Jobs and the Economy

Conservation ◀ ▬ ▬ ▬ ▬ ▬ ▬ ▬ ▬ ▶ Convenience

Conserve Water ◀ ▬ ▬ ▬ ▬ ▬ ▬ ▬ ▬ ▶ Affordable Electricity

However, if we instead take a *complex systems approach* and identify the polarities, we consider the interconnectedness of things, and how a change in one area will affect all other areas. It's only then that we can begin to balance the needs, make tough but intentional and informed choices between the values, and prioritize in a way that takes everyone into account. It's true in this example, and true for all of our shared, Wicked Problems. Collaboration and negotiation will be key to moving forward in the 21st century.[7]

Polarization in Society is Exaggerated

A few years ago, I was so frustrated (like many of you) by the polarization I saw around me and that I experienced with my friends and peers. Happily, discovering Clare W. Graves and the different layers of value systems he described gave me some context and comfort about what was happening. I'll explain more in later chapters, but I was also fascinated (and shocked!) to learn that we're *not* as polarized as many of us think.

While our times feel extreme, we *have* been here before. Humans have evolved from one dominant value layer to the next, again and again throughout our history. Societies, companies, and groups all have a dominant value system that's based on the relative population level and power of people currently holding each of the existing value systems. When enough people transition into a value system layer, it becomes the dominant layer for their society. The transition between these layers doesn't happen overnight. It can actually take years, even decades (or longer). It's also difficult to know the exact moment when the shift happens. However, a seemingly inevitable part of the process of that transition is a rise in polarization between the existing and emerging value system layers.

Dr. Don Beck, a developmental psychologist, has spent most of his life applying The Change Code to some of the highest tension places in the world, including South Africa and the Middle East. While writing this book, I had the pleasure of spending time and becoming friends with Dr. Beck.

We connected immediately over our shared interest in Graves' theories, and our drive to decrease polarization and bring more peace to the planet. I am still in awe of Dr. Beck's commitment to this work. When he met Graves, Beck was a full professor at the University of North Texas. Even though he was raising a family, Dr. Beck knew he had to apply the model to the toughest conflicts in the world. So, he left his position and headed to South Africa to work with Nelson Mandela, primarily funding the work himself with his retirement savings.

Beck told me that he had studied the factors that contributed to the American Civil War, the bloodiest war in U.S. history, prior to working with Graves. The stories of the battles and mass casualties sustained by both sides were dreadful enough to the young Beck that he committed his life to preventing future wars. This also inspired his trips to South Africa.

As we chatted for hours in his living room, I learned that he is even more concerned about the world now than he was back in the 1990s. He said that the levels of polarization today correspond to those between the North and South in mid-19th Century America. Just before the Civil War broke out. Imagine that.

James Lo, assistant professor of political science at the USC Dornsife College of Letters, Arts, and Sciences, agrees that our country is as polarized now as it was just before the Civil War began. Lo's work measures legislators' positions on the spectrum of liberal to conservative based on their roll call voting records. The scores suggest that the US is as polarized today as it was then. However, there's also a huge group in the middle that both of our political parties fail to represent.[8]

Lo's work is supported by research from The American Political Science Association's (APSA) Task Force on Negotiating Agreement in Politics. They found that most voters are moderates when it comes to their policy positions. In studies comparing voter positions to legislator positions, legislative representatives were found to be considerably more extreme than their constituents.[9]

Another study by a group of researchers from More in Common found similar results in their large-scale survey of more than 8,000 Americans. More in Common is an international initiative to build societies and communities that are stronger, more united, and more resilient to the increasing threats of polarization and social division.

In 2018, they issued a report called, "Hidden Tribes, A Study of America's Polarized Landscape"[10] that summarized the results of their survey.

In talking to everyday Americans, we have found a large segment of the population whose voices are rarely heard above the shouts of the partisan tribes. These are people who believe that Americans have more in common than that which divides them. While they differ on important issues, they feel exhausted by the division in the United States. They believe that compromise is necessary in politics, as in other parts of life, and want to see the country come together and solve its problems." These individuals are shown below as the "exhausted majority."

THE HIDDEN TRIBES OF AMERICA

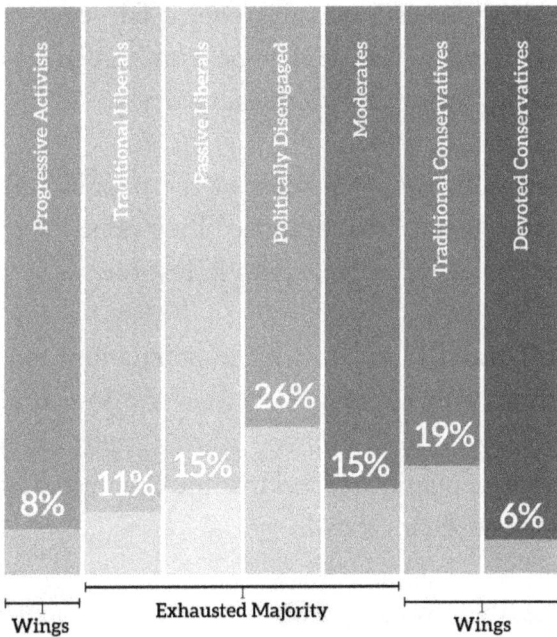

Progressive Activists 8% · Traditional Liberals 11% · Passive Liberals 15% · Politically Disengaged 26% · Moderates 15% · Traditional Conservatives 19% · Devoted Conservatives 6%

Wings — Exhausted Majority — Wings

Used with permission from www.hiddentribes.us

This chart shows that, despite America's profound polarization, the middle (which is labeled the "Exhausted Majority") is far larger than conventional wisdom suggests. And the strident wings of progressivism and conservatism are far smaller. Progressive Activists are not representative of most liberal Americans, Devoted Conservatives are not representative of most conservative Americans. Yet everyone seems to see only a caricature of the other side.

Here's a quick snapshot of each group from HiddenTribes:[11]

Progressive Activists (8 percent of the population) are deeply concerned with issues concerning equity, fairness, and America's direction today. They tend to be more secular, cosmopolitan, and highly engaged with social media.

Traditional Liberals (11 percent of the population) tend to be cautious, rational, and idealistic. They value tolerance and compromise. They place great faith in institutions.

Passive Liberals (15 percent of the population) tend to feel isolated from their communities. They are insecure in their beliefs and try to avoid political conversations. They have a fatalistic view of politics and feel that the circumstances of their lives are beyond their control.

The Politically Disengaged (26 percent of the population) are untrusting, suspicious about external threats, conspiratorially minded, and pessimistic about progress. They tend to be patriotic yet detached from politics.

Moderates (15 percent of the population) are engaged in their communities, well informed, and civic-minded. Their faith is often an important part of their lives. They shy away from extremism of any sort.

Traditional Conservatives (19 percent of the population) tend to be religious, patriotic, and highly moralistic. They believe deeply in personal responsibility and self-reliance.

Devoted Conservatives (6 percent of the population) are deeply engaged with politics and hold strident, uncompromising views. They feel that America is embattled, and they perceive themselves as the last defenders of traditional values that are under threat.

Our news media promotes these differences. They feature individuals with extreme views, in search of clicks and ratings. This creates the impression that the outliers are typical and represent the majority. And this in turn leads to the Exaggerated Polarization that we'll discuss shortly.

As a result of people becoming exhausted (the Exhausted Majority) by politics, most of our Wicked Problems have fallen into the extreme wings of politics. This means that issues such as healthcare, education, violence, and climate change have landed in the hands of extremists, making it difficult to pull these problems back into a collaborative space for finding cooperative solutions.

EXERCISE BOX:

Where do you fall on the political spectrum? Take the free assessment at HiddenTribes.us.

When you get your results, take a moment to reflect and possibly even journal your responses to the following questions:

❖ What is at the heart of your political beliefs?

❖ What in your life experiences has led you to believe the things you do?

❖ What are your earliest memories of political discussions in your home, school, church, or community?

❖ Do these beliefs still align with the person you would like to be? Why or why not?

Divided We Fall: The Vicious Cycle of Exaggerated Polarization

All of this leads us to our current state—a vicious cycle of exaggerated polarization that is preventing us from working together on the most urgent problems facing the world.

Our political parties have drifted too far apart, with Republican politicians moving much further to the right and Democratic politicians moving to the left. Even though most people's beliefs aren't as extreme as our politicians, our tribalistic nature causes us to align with our political party and creates subconscious biases.

The news media makes the division worse by focusing its reporting on those with extreme viewpoints, in an attempt to increase views and likes. The negative portrayal of both sides creates a negative interaction effect by confirming our subconscious biases. Let's look at this cycle in the following diagram.

THE VICIOUS CYCLE OF EXAGGERATED POLARIZATION

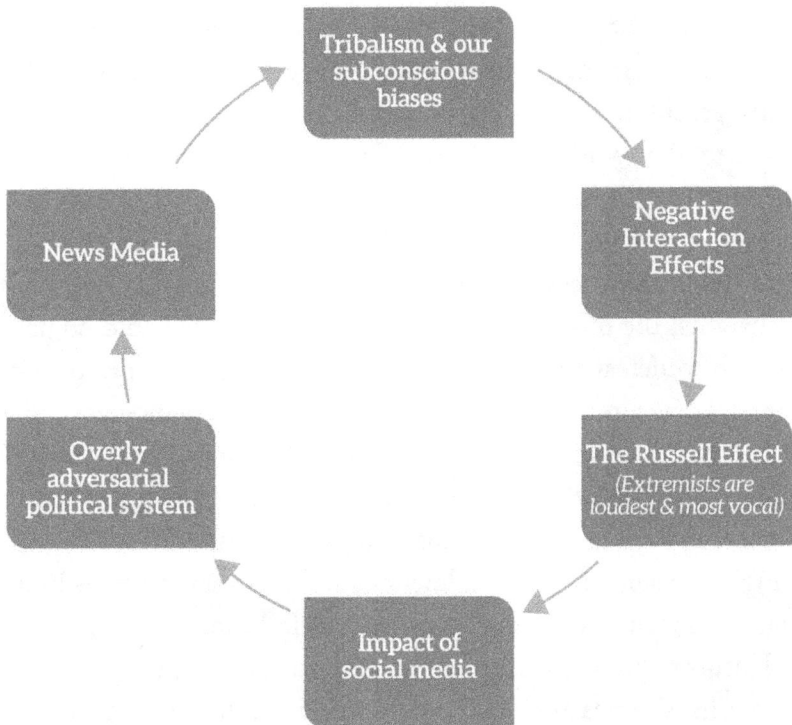

Tribalism & our subconscious biases

Negative Interaction Effects

The Russell Effect *(Extremists are loudest & most vocal)*

Impact of social media

Overly adversarial political system

News Media

Our Political System is Overly Adversarial

So, while it may be a relief to know the average voter has not become much more polarized, our political parties have. Unfortunately, the middle has no home in either the Republican or the Democratic party. Our two-party system tends to accommodate those at both ends of the spectrum, but it comes at the expense of the middle.

In reviewing the literature, I found this movement of the political parties toward the extremes over the past forty years did not happen equally on both sides. Instead, there is a far greater shift of the Republican party to the right on most issues, including economics. However, in social issues such as gay marriage, Democrats have moved to the left.[12]

The differences in our political parties have resulted in increased tribalization. Gender, sexual orientation, religion, race, and ethnicity are essential to who we are, and often determine the tribe we choose to align with. Tribalism is fueled by a culture of outrage and offense-taking. It's easy to see this when you look at social media, read the comments section to almost any news story, or even scan the headlines at the checkout counter of your local supermarket. For the combatants, the other side can no longer be tolerated, and no price is too high to defeat them. These tensions are poisoning personal relationships, consuming our politics, and putting our democracy in peril.

More and more, people feel isolated and begin to see themselves as separate from the whole. While this may feel initially like freedom, it also creates feelings of alienation and hopelessness. As a result, we're seeing more suicide, opioid addiction, and mass shootings as individuals experiencing these extreme emotions fall over the edge.

Unsurprisingly, our in-progress move into the next layer of development in America also creates stress and uncertainty for those still in the previous layers. They feel their value systems are being threatened and their core beliefs are being called into question. To cope, people reach out to and align more closely with their specific belief groups, which is why we see the rise in tribalism.

CHANGE CODE IN ACTION

NPR HOSTED AN INTERVIEW in October 2018 that illustrates the differences in values in two communities. One is progressive (Green in this case, which we'll cover in Chapter 3, although progressive is not always Green), the other conservative (Blue in this case, although conservative is not always Blue). See if you can guess which is which:

1. The schools in Community A stress patriotism and respect; it's a very rules-based educational system. The houses are fairly similar with nicely-kept green lawns are nicely kept, and a beautiful green. The town is quiet, with lots of churches.

2. The schools in Community B are based on experiential learning rather than rote memory. People prefer older houses with wooden floors rather than wall-to-wall carpeting. They keep the yards natural. There are more bars and community theaters than churches.

The first description is from a conservative (Blue) lens that prefers order. The second is from a progressive (Green) lens that prefers ambiguity. Do you see how a person might align with one or the other from a tribal perspective? You probably found yourself attracted to one of the two communities.

The point of these examples isn't to stereotype anyone, but to show how our political beliefs often flow from subconscious value systems.[13]

The Russell Effect

No surprise, the most politically polarized individuals are the most active ones in politics. This amplifies their voices and makes it more challenging for parties to meet each other halfway. I probably don't need to give examples here as you see this every time you turn on the TV or look at social media.

> "The whole problem with the world is that fools and fanatics are always so certain of themselves, and wiser people so full of doubts."
>
> — *Bertrand Russell*

Some political scientists call this the "Russell Effect" after Bertrand Russell and his famous quote, "The whole problem with the world is that fools and fanatics are always so certain of themselves, and wiser people so full of doubts."[14]

The Role of the News Media

And then there's the news media—I could write an entire book on that alone! The advent of cable television and rise of the Internet have changed our news landscape completely. Specialized news shows cater specifically to one party or the other, which shifts the views of voters. Journalists focus on sensationalized versions of what's actually happening in the world, and the popularity of stories (based on clicks) determines how and when stories appear in our personal news feeds.

The changes in media over the past 30 years have also contributed to polarization. Before the Internet and cable television, traditional news provided a consensus for reality. There were strict journalistic ethics and standards, and the primary sources of news were newspapers and large media outlets. While this unfortunately led to certain voices being silenced and certain stories remaining untold, it nevertheless meant the whole country heard the same overall set of facts and shared agreement on the overall narrative.

The emergence of the Internet and cable television democratized the news. Fast forward to now and anyone with a phone can immediately broadcast a video, blog post, or tweet with any viewpoint, based in fact or not. As a result, the lines between the news media and social media have become blurred, and people seem to be losing the ability to differentiate facts from opinions.

Cable television brought with it 24-hour channels with multiple options for news, creating two very distinct general experiences. Fox News has become the source for conservative media, lightening the responsibilities of journalists with their philosophy of "We Report. You Decide." CNN and MSNBC are widely regarded as the sources for liberal media, even though studies generally place MSNBC on the left with CNN falling mostly in the middle. Viewers of these networks are generally exposed to the same stories, but with irreconcilable interpretations and different sets of "facts."

Today, instead of informing the public and being an objective voice, profit-driven news media serves to exacerbate tribalism through competition and contributes to our polarization. As a result, more people distrust the news, or avoid it altogether.

Effects of Exaggerated Polarization

Once a country is internally tribalized, debates about contested issues from immigration and trade to economic management, climate change, and national security, are all seen through the lens of tribal identities. Policy debate gives way to tribal conflicts.

Recently, a walkout by Republican legislators in Oregon over a bill that would limit carbon emissions made worldwide headlines. Democrats have an 18 to 12 majority in the Oregon Senate and put forth a bill that aimed to dramatically reduce greenhouse gases by 2050, by capping carbon emissions and requiring businesses to buy or trade for pollution allowances. California currently has a similar cap and trade program.[15]

When Republican legislators walked out rather than vote, the Governor sent out the state police to find them, though many had left the state. One senator even threatened the state police and received a formal complaint from the Senate Special Committee on Conduct.[16]

If it all seems a little like a modern-day episode of "Gunsmoke" to you, you're not alone. I think it's safe to say that neither side demonstrated the type of collaboration that we expect from our representatives. The end result? No action was taken to begin limiting carbon emissions, or to begin addressing the issue of climate change. While Republicans in Oregon might have chalked this stalemate up to a win, in the end, humanity and the environment only suffer more.

In a polarized society, the focus moves to winning as opposed to actually solving problems. One side blames the other and avoids taking responsibility. The most extreme voices get amplified.

> Because we aren't working on solutions, our problems will only become more complex.

We are spending more and more time just managing the polarization and the end results of government shutdowns, stalemates, and culture wars waged by folks with different value systems. And with some of our problems, like climate change, our time to come together is limited.

In response to these power struggles, several scientists are studying the negative impacts of polarization, and how too much polarity can severely damage or destroy democracy.

Our political leaders play an important role in polarization and the increase in tribalism. Jennifer Lynn McCoy, professor of political science at Georgia State University, studied 11 countries including the U.S., Turkey, Hungary, Venezuela, and Thailand. She found that when political leaders cast their opponents as "immoral" or "corrupt," they created "us" and "them" camps. This tactic plays to our tribalistic nature.

Each side begins to view the other as an "out group" with increasing distrust and polarization on issues, even when the individuals may not actually be that far apart.

This can be seen in the conflict surrounding Obamacare and the many efforts to repeal that set of laws. It's amazing that fully 35 percent of poll respondents didn't understand that Obamacare is just another name for the Affordable Care Act, which oddly enjoys higher levels of support when referred to by its official title.[17]

Tribalism is based in a zero-sum mentality: "If you win, I lose." Each side views the other political party and their supporters as a threat to the nation or their way of life. This is the root cause of the Wicked Problems we discussed above.

Tribalism causes us to align with individuals and actions that we might not otherwise support. Can you think of an example of this?

For that reason, the incumbent's followers tolerate more illiberal and increasingly authoritarian behavior to stay in power, while the opponents are more and more willing to resort to undemocratic means to remove them from power. This damages democracy.[18]

We are already seeing these divides in the United States. Twenty-seven percent of Democrats and 36 percent of Republicans see the other party as "a threat to the nation's well-being," according to a 2014 Pew Research study. And those considered "consistent" liberals and conservatives feel even more threatened. Among those who hold uniform liberal or conservative beliefs, 50 percent of liberals and 66 percent of conservatives see the other side as a threat to the nation.[19]

In summary

When it feels like there's no end in sight to the arguments, blaming, and bad-mouthing, remember that polarization is a natural result of change, and an inevitable part of a major paradigm shift. Once enough people move into the next value system layer, change will happen very quickly. We are nearing the tipping point.

What it's going to take from here is action. As a change leader, you're a light who will help guide others through the shift to a better place for mankind and the planet. In this book, I'll share practical tips and things you can personally do now and continue throughout your life to contribute to society as a whole.

You'll soon understand how to guide groups or organizations you lead, start and improve conversations with people who have different views, and help yourself, so you continue to grow and thrive through change.

But first, let's talk a bit about how change happens, and learn about those different value layers.

CHAPTER 2

How Change Really Happens

Every great dream begins with a dreamer.
Always remember, you have within you the strength, the patience,
and the passion to reach for the stars to change the world.
~HARRIET TUBMAN

What if I told you there is an underlying pattern for human change? That there is an order to our development as individuals and as a society?

If there is an underlying pattern, that means change can be predictable, and that if change is predictable, we might create a roadmap to help explain the past and show us a path forward for the future.

Imagine what we could do with something like that—solve today's biggest problems like the fires in the Amazon and Greenland's melting ice sheath, get in front of future and emerging issues, and help humans and society evolve more quickly and with less conflict? We could also help ourselves and our families feel more at ease in the world as we identify opportunities to make the world a better place.

You might feel a bit skeptical, frightened, or excited about the potential. And those are exactly the feelings I had when I first learned of Clare W. Graves and his groundbreaking discovery of the pattern for human development.

The more I learned about Spiral Dynamics, the more I saw its potential to help leaders accelerate positive transformation on the planet. This tool has already been applied in some of the world's most challenging hotspots and small towns in rural America alike—to ease tensions and bring people together.

Graves' theory provides context for the polarization we see in today's society. His layers explain deep-rooted values that drive how individuals think. It's important to note that his theory describes *systems within people*, and *not types of people*.

Graves gave his theory the catchy name of "**Emergent, Cyclical, Double Helix Model of Adult Biopsychosocial Development**." When asked about the mouthful of a name during a presentation, he told the audience, *"I'm sorry, but that's what it is!"*

Bear with me here. I promise this will make sense! Breaking down this lengthy theory name helps explain the underlying premises of the theory as follows:

Emergent – development progresses from simple to more complex stages.

Cyclical – patterns repeat and build on one another. Like layers of an onion, as we evolve we develop new capacities while previous capacities are still there in the layers below.

Double Helix –two parallel strands are of equal importance in our development —our life conditions and the adaptive nature of our consciousness.

Adult – this research focused on adults; however, the stages are parallel with childhood developmental stages.

Biopsychosocial development – there is a mind-body connection and the mind is shaped by neurological structures and networks while also being activated by chemical interactions and one's life conditions. At the time, this was heresy in the scientific world, but Graves held fast. Research today supports his conclusions.

Today, neuroscientists have discovered that the brain is constantly changing, even in adulthood; this process is known as neuroplasticity. We learn new facts, skills, and perspectives; and all this learning is, ultimately, encoded in the brain's neural connections.

When we perform a new task or think in a new way, we form new neural connections. If we continue to repeat these tasks, the new pathways in our brain get stronger and faster over time. Through our own actions and habits, we can literally rewire our brains, which allows us to grow and change. This naturally occurring process is demonstrated in Graves' model.

Are you still with me?

Thankfully, this theory was given the much simpler name "Spiral Dynamics" by Graves' student and colleague Don Beck, along with Christopher Cowan, a student of Beck's. In their book, *Spiral Dynamics: Mastering Values, Leadership and Change*, they outline Graves' work and tell how they used the model.

So how did a mild-mannered psychologist from Schenectady develop this theory that has world-changing potential?

In his classes at Union College, Graves regularly taught five different developmental psychology theories. When his students asked him which one was the most accurate, he couldn't give them an answer. So he set out to find one. To do this, he studied a huge array of "change theories" from psychology, economics, religion, and systems. He wanted to understand the underlying pattern for human change.

What Constitutes a Healthy Adult?

According to Beck, Graves wanted to know "What is the system maker, what is it in human nature that triggers major shifts or regressions, and how can we understand the dynamics of change." **In simpler terms, he was looking to define what constitutes a healthy adult.**[20]

Starting in 1954, Graves spent nine years doing field research, interviewing, observing, and testing more than 1,000 individuals. He spent the next 20 years analyzing the data.

Graves had health problems for many years before his death in 1986, and was never able to publish his work. This meant that his theory was never peer-reviewed, did not get the recognition it deserved at the time, and isn't taught in mainstream psychology. This is why, though his ground-breaking work has been successfully used around the world, many people still haven't heard of Clare W. Graves. Many others have gone on to validate Graves' conclusions, however.

In fact, Ken Wilber, the well-known founder of the Integral movement which incorporates Spiral Dynamics, emphasized that the Gravesian model has so far "been tested in more than fifty thousand people from around the world, and there have been no major exceptions found in the general scheme."[21]

The theory has gained traction in recent years as our society goes through another major shift and people are seeking solutions. That's because this theory provides context for the transition, helps us understand the past, and gives us hope for the future.

Before I go into Graves' model, there's something I want you to know: These operations are nearly all unconscious. In fact, up to 98 percent of our thoughts are unconscious.[22]

By studying The Change Code, however, we can become more conscious about how our brain works and affects our worldview, and why we do what we do.

A Theory of Everything

Graves discovered the underlying pattern for human and societal change and the sequence of stages that we all move through, also known as Spiral Dynamics, or what I call "The Change Code." In the late 1960s, *Maclean's* Magazine referred to his concept as "the theory that explains everything." While Graves would cringe at such a broad statement about his work, it does indeed act as a unifying framework that applies to a single individual, an organization, or an entire society.[23]

Here's how The Change Code works:

1. **We Evolve Through a Sequence of Defined Layers.**
   Graves discovered that human and societal values aren't fixed; they evolve through a series of layers. These layers follow the same pattern for everyone and are sequential and predictable.

   Layers come in phases, like waves to a beach. A layer first emerges on a small scale (ENTERING), then it will have its ascending surge until it reaches its peak (PEAK), then it will break and recede. Finally, it will fade into the background (EXITING) while being replaced by another, for that moment more dominant, layer.

   And, here's what is so fascinating: Everyone goes through the same layers of consciousness in exactly the same order. Layers can't be skipped. And there are both positive and negative expressions for the values at each level. I'll get into the layers later on.

2. **Layers Are Determined by Life Conditions.**
   Our consciousness layer and view of the world are directly related to the complexity of our life conditions. We form deep value systems in each layer. These value systems are unconscious and determine *how* we think (not *what* we think).

   For example, if your world view is that we live in a dangerous place and you must protect yourself at all times, you will view the situation very differently than someone who believes that the Universe is conspiring for our good.

Take the issue of gun control for example. This is a bit extreme, but if you deeply believe the world is a dangerous place, you may think any regulation of gun ownership takes away your ability to protect yourself. However, if you believe the Universe conspires for your good, you may naturally think guns aren't necessary for the average person and we'd be better off with fewer guns on the street.

3. **Development to the Next Layer is an Adaptation to Life's Growing Complexity.**

   As our life conditions become more complex— as we have kids, take on bigger work challenges, need more money, get more education, etc.—we adapt to that complexity in order to survive. This adaptation happens on the neurological, psychological, and social levels. Changing life conditions is the impetus for human and societal change.

4. **Layers Are Cumulative.**

   When we move to a new layer, it transcends and includes the lower layers, and this allows us to access all that we learned in the previous layers. The process is like an onion growing a new layer, or a student moving from fourth grade to fifth grade. It's often compared to a nested Russian doll. As a new layer emerges, the previous layer is nested inside the new one.

5. **Layers Alternate Between a *Me* Focus and a *We* Focus and a *Left* and a *Right* Brain Dominance.**

   As consciousness evolves it swings back and forth between two poles of "me" and "we." Each new layer, then, is a kind of reaction or correction for the extremes of the existing layer. Too much "me" consciousness causes a new layer of "we" consciousness to emerge, and vice versa. Think of how we moved from the peace-and-love 1960s right into the get-all-you-can-get-now 80s.

The "me" or individual layers primarily access the left side of the brain while the "we" or collective layers primarily access the right side of the brain with the following characteristics:

Left Brain (me)	Right Brain (we)
Linear	Big Picture
Logical	Gestalt
Structured	Creative
Detailed Oriented	Nature
Science	Relationships
Rational	Having Fun

People have the ability to access both sides of the brain in an integrated fashion, for a whole brain experience once they reach a certain (Yellow) layer.

6. **Not Everyone (or every society) is at the Same Layer**
An individual expresses multiple layers at the same time, although the layer with the most complexity will be dominant. Going back to our old analogy, think of the onion. Onions and humans each have many layers. New layers simply grow over the existing layers, giving us access to the earlier layers when needed.

A society is made up of individuals in the full spectrum of layers as well, although one layer will be dominant. Humans and societies are complex and the movement from one layer to the next can take years or even decades. It is also possible, and natural, for individuals and societies to regress to an earlier layer as part of the change process.

Our life conditions affect the expression of the layers. For example, a person with a high-level corporate job spends her days expressing at a certain layer to be successful at work. When she gets home to her kids, she may express a different layer.

7. **One Primary Layer is Typically the Strongest, and, Different Aspects of Our Personality Develop at Different Times.**
Wilber and Beck identified 13 "streams" of development. These streams include emotional, kinesthetic, morality, creativity, aesthetics, gender, sexuality, empathy, relational, cognitive, spiritual, contemplative, and political. Individuals may be at different layers in these areas, however one color will be dominant across most streams.

For example, if you were raised in a very rigid, rules-based environment where you weren't allowed to express your creativity, your creativity may be a different layer than other aspects of your development.

As you begin to study The Change Code, you will notice these different aspects of yourself and various expressions of the layers that we'll cover in the next chapter.

8. **Layer Differences Between Individuals Result in Fear and Judgment, Both of Which are Unproductive.**
It is human nature to reject our previous layer and even judge those who remain in that layer. If you are thinking that you don't judge, picture someone on the other side of the gun control issue or the abortion issue. Feel any judgement?

We also tend to fear the behaviors and beliefs of the higher layers. This creates tension and conflict between the layers.

The exception to this is once an individual or society reaches the seventh (or yellow) layer of consciousness, where an appreciation for the value of all layers develops. I'll describe this in detail in Chapter 3.

9. **Differences in Value Systems (i.e., Layers) Cause Conflict Between People and Cultures.**
    This difference in layers is a difference in core values, which creates tension and conflict. And this is *exactly* what our world is experiencing right now.

10. **Polarization Within Layers Can Also Cause Conflict.**
    It is possible for individuals operating from the same layer to have conflicts, such as individuals from different religions. Think of the Middle East where several groups in the same primary layer hold very different beliefs about how a society should be structured.

> Understanding this framework leads to deep and meaningful solutions, both for individuals and for the world.

As I've mentioned, Graves' theory has been used to ease some of the most difficult conflicts in the world, including apartheid in South Africa. It's been called *A Theory of Everything* because it can be applied to *any* human or societal situation.

One more thing before we really jump in.

Graves vs. Maslow and Maslow's Hierarchy of Needs

Graves was a peer of Abraham Maslow, best known for his Hierarchy of Needs. If you've taken any introductory psychology class, chances are you've studied this theory and you may have wondered as you've read about The Change Code if there's any similarity.

MASLOW'S HIERARCHY OF NEEDS

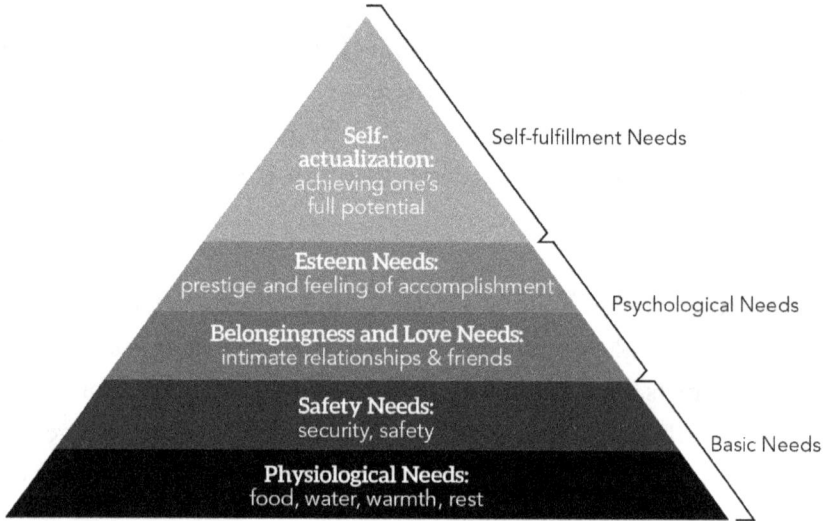

According to Maslow, once basic physiological needs like food, water, and safety are met, humans can focus on their psychological needs like love and creating a feeling of belonging. If humans continue to work and evolve through these stages, Maslow believed, they will eventually reach a stage of self-actualization where all of their needs are met and they feel a deep sense of fulfillment.

Graves was fond of Maslow, but he was troubled by limitations he found with the model. For instance, the Hierarchy of Needs is a closed model, with a clear beginning and end. In Graves' research, there is *no end* to human development. For Graves, nature is ever-changing and so are we. We will continue to move into new and more complex layers as long as we exist as a species. Graves also found self-actualized people at every layer of his model. While Maslow believed our growth primarily comes from within, Graves held that external factors were crucial to our development.

⌒

So, is the goal of Graves' model to move through all the different layers during our lifetime? Not necessarily.

According to Graves, we can find fulfillment in any layer. What's more important is our ability to adapt to our current environment and circumstances. In fact, he found this adaptability to be the deciding factor for living a successful life.

Graves believed that there is no upper limit:

*As he sets off on each quest, he believes he will find the answer to his existence. Yet, much to his surprise and much to his dismay, he finds at every stage that the solution to existence is not the solution he has come to find. Every stage he reaches leaves him disconcerted and perplexed. It is simply that as he solves one set of human problems, he finds a new set in their place. **The quest he finds is never ending.**[24]*

How Change Really Happens

As our world gets more and more complex, we begin to encounter new types of problems. When the problems get so complex that our existing systems and coping mechanisms are no longer effective, our life conditions change.

This can cause us to feel stress. The things we knew for sure about the world are no longer true and our solutions no longer work. It feels chaotic. Have you been feeling that lately?

All it takes is looking at the headlines, the regular articles about sex scandals in the Catholic Church, religious and other leaders falling from grace, news alerts about the poisons in our food and water, drug companies taking advantage of patients who desperately need their medication, and the disappearance of basic civil behavior online.

Here's the thing. Change requires dissonance; just having an insight isn't enough for us to change as we still have to overcome barriers from the old layer. And we don't change when we're complacent and life is smooth sailing.

To move out of the chaos, we have to gain new perspectives and look at the world differently to find ways to solve these new problems. Once we identify new and effective solutions and coping skills, our life begins to stabilize again. And in the process, we gain new insights and tools that we often want to share with others. Many will become evangelists during this time and want to help others navigate the chaos. Have you ever had a friend discover a new yoga practice or political candidate and she can't stop talking about it?

Finally, we reach a new normal or layer of stability. The layer is higher than our previous layer. Graves broke this process into five steps.

Stable Phase:

You've reached a layer of normalcy and things seem to be going along fine. The one consistency in life is change, though, so the stable phase doesn't last forever.

Tension Phase:

Everything seems stable—but you realize one day that you're unhappy and you're not sure why. This discomfort doesn't go away and begins to cause stress and dissatisfaction, you are experiencing a values crisis. The root cause is the current layer has become oppressive, although that's not obvious at first. The environment has become more complex. You feel a sense of turbulence that rocks your boat.

The stress causes you to look back through your life to remember when things were going well and when you didn't feel the stress. When things are chaotic, you want to revert back to a simpler world view to try to find comfort and stability again. This is why you hear things like "Make America Great Again" and the "Good Ol' Days."

Now, here's where it gets interesting. This regressive search only increases the tension you are experiencing, creating an even stronger

THE CHANGE PROCESS

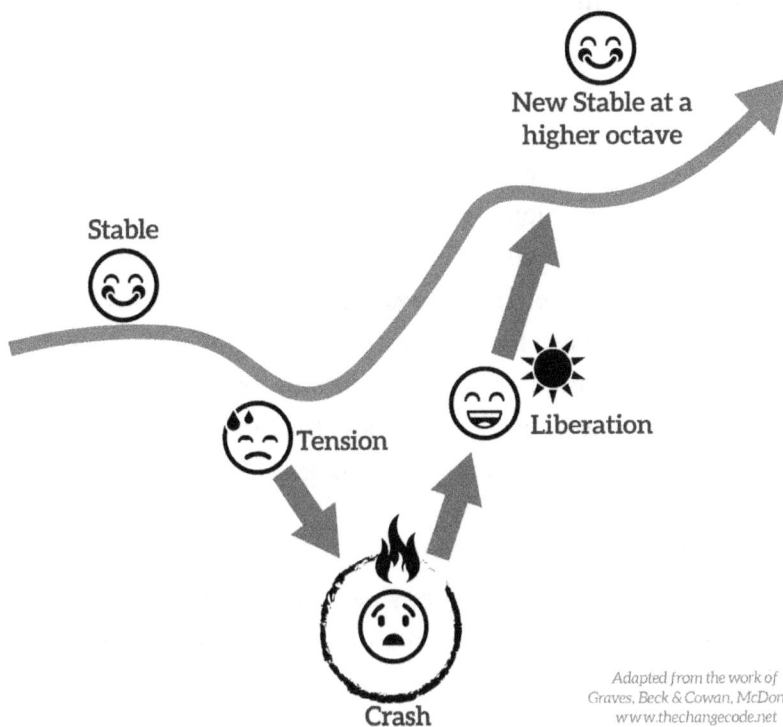

New Stable at a higher octave

Stable

Tension

Liberation

Crash

Adapted from the work of
Graves, Beck & Cowan, McDonald
www.thechangecode.net

impetus for change. Reverting back to a simpler time can't happen. The world has changed and the circumstances have become too complex. The old ways don't work and, eventually, you realize you must change.

Crash Phase:
So just like a rubber band that's been pulled back, enough tension builds up that it has to be released. The tension pushes you forward into uncharted waters that can feel stressful and chaotic. You feel a "crash" as your current ways of coping with the challenges are no longer effective. It may even feel like your entire world is falling apart.

Exiting the crash phase requires new insights and a breakthrough, which is why this process is sometimes referred to as a "Revolutionary Change." The insights are the metaphorical light bulb moments, or the light at the end of the tunnel that leads you out of the Crash. Over time, you begin to find your way through the feelings of chaos, and move to liberation.

Liberation Phase:
You are now able to fully develop the new coping mechanisms that you need for your life conditions and fully integrate them into your life. You adapt to your new environment and conditions and see the world through a new perspective. This allows you to remove any environmental barriers that have been holding you back. Because of the success in navigating the chaos and finding new solutions, some individuals will evangelize the solutions they found in an effort to help others. If this change is significant, you will move to the next layer.

New Stable Phase
After Liberation, you move into our new normal. But this phase is at a higher octave and complexity than your previous stability phase. Don't get too comfortable. You get to enjoy the stability phase for a while until your life conditions change and then the process starts over again.[25]

To illustrate these phases, let's look at alcoholism and recovery.

Stable: You enjoy having cocktails at dinner parties and occasionally on the weekends.

Tension: You've increased your drinking from parties and on the weekends to a daily practice. Having a strong cocktail at the end of a long day has become the highlight and you can't wait for work to be over so you can have a drink.

Crash: You're no longer able to wait until you get home to have a drink. You're now having cocktails during your lunch hour and sneaking a drink or two during the day. Your boss finds out and you get fired from your job. Your spouse and family are angry with you and you just got a DUI. There's no denying you have a problem and things have to change. You take the first step for change and begin attending Alcoholics Anonymous (AA) meetings.

Liberation: You realize that you weren't managing your stress well and are now learning new breathing, prayer, and meditation techniques. You've been attending AA meetings for more than a year. Your new breathing techniques and stress coping mechanisms are helping and you feel great. You become an Evangelist for these techniques and eagerly share them with others.

New Stable: You're back to life in your new normal. You go to work, spend time with your family, continue your routines, and life is good.

How the Change Code Worked in the Industrial Revolution

The Change Code isn't new—it's as old as humanity. In the 18th & 19th centuries, humans evolved from an agrarian society into an industrial one. As life conditions became much more complex, many people moved from farms into cities.

The focus had been solely on agriculture—sustenance and wealth came from the land. People produced the bulk of their own food, clothing, and tools. They were likely part of a community church and followed strict rules and routines. Then came the Industrial Revolution, in which technology enabled mass production and required external energy sources, such as fossil fuels, to increase the rate and scale of production.

The ability to purchase goods—versus the ability to produce crops— began to define an individual's worth. Communication, transportation, government, and banking all changed to support this new economic model. What was so familiar on the farm was different in the city. They had to create and adapt to new, more complex systems. If you were used to gathering eggs and picking beans for your meals, can you imagine how stressful and even chaotic it would have felt to suddenly be navigating a streetcar to get to the bank and grocery store?

Some of the signs of that stress were protests, including attacks on factories and the destruction of machinery in 19ᵗʰ century England. The attackers, called "Luddites" after their leader Ned Ludd, feared the changes that were happening. The term is still used for those who oppose technological advancements.

As most people adapted to their new life conditions, their perspective began to change as well. Their underlying value system began to align with their new world. It's also human nature to want to abandon the previous stage, even though it had plenty of positive attributes. For many years, it was no longer desirable to make your own clothes or grow your own food, after all, there were factories that could do that now.

This is an example of our society moving between two layers in Graves' model, from the Blue layer to the Orange layer. I'll explain more about the individual layers and their corresponding colors later in the next chapter.

Our society is undergoing a similar change now and many feel stressed, uncomfortable, and chaotic. This also explains why there is such incredible polarization between groups in different layers.

While the majority of society moved into the industrial age, a new phase in human development, not everyone changed together. Some farmers stayed in the country holding to their traditional worldview.

While it's natural to shun the past layer when we've moved past it, it's important to remember that regardless of the dominant layer for society as a whole, there will always be individuals at every layer; this is normal.

A Layers Recap

The layers of the Change Code determine **how** we think but not **what** we think, and are based on the conditions in which we live. Each layer is important; happens in the same, predictable order for every person; and can't be skipped. Both individuals and societies go through the layers.

We don't always progress forward. When necessary for survival, we can regress back to earlier layers. It's also possible to get stuck or just comfortable in one layer, for years, or even decades until life conditions propel us forward.

Things like poverty, illness, helplessness, and social rejection can also slow or even reverse human growth and development. Some reach a certain layer, usually around age 25, and remain there for the rest of their lives, or until around mid-life, a time that often prompts change. If someone's life conditions don't demand change, there isn't anything that prompts them to change. They may be perfectly fine where they are, and that's ok.

Layers go from the less complex to more complex. Each layer builds on the previous layer and includes all of the previous layers within it. Ken Wilber coined the term "transcend & include" to describe this process. Again, think of humans like Russian dolls—each layer is whole and complete and exists intact within the other layers.

Layers also alternate between left-brain and right-brain emphasis, until we reach the Second Tier (which we'll discuss soon), where we finally have a whole brain focus.

This left to right and upward movement creates the shape of a spiral, a common form in nature (think of ferns, seashells, tornados, the Milky Way, and our own DNA). That is why Don Beck and Christopher Cowan renamed the theory as Spiral Dynamics.

And because it is evenly distributed across all layers, intelligence is not a factor. Individuals can have the same level of intelligence at every layer. In other words, you don't need to be smarter to progress, and people in earlier layers are not less intelligent in any way.

The time societies spend in each layer decreases over time. Humans spent thousands of years at the early layers of development (Beige, Red) but the time between the layers has been decreasing. Like me, you may have felt that we are moving much more quickly now. As our communication technology has improved, we have gone from handwritten letters, to telegraphs, to telephones, and now to email, instant messaging, and the Internet. We now have access to a world of information on our smart phones. The more information that's available creates more complexity, spurring the need for faster change.

If our environment is at a higher layer, it will pull us up. If it is at a lower layer, it will pull us down.

It's natural to look down on those in the layers below and throw out elements from the earlier stages, even the good parts, while at the same time fearing things from the next layers. They challenge our thinking, and most importantly, our values and beliefs about the world. This is why it's so difficult to move between layers, especially when we are comfortable where we are.

And it's not just about our ideas about things. When we do move to a new layer, it affects our *physiology*, and our brain adapts. Thank you, neuroplasticity! Our neural wiring allows us to change, redirect, and rewire our brains through our attitudes, actions, habits, and emotions. For instance, when we move from the pre-rational layers (beige, purple, red) to the rational layers, the pre-frontal cortex of the brain becomes more activated. The development of our pre-frontal cortex allows us to increase our abstract thoughts and reason with more complexity and forethought. It also allows us to moderate and overrule our pre-rational urges when necessary.

Within each layer, we experience learning differently and have different perceptions of time. For example, a homeless person who's focused on food, shelter, and survival (this is the Beige layer, which I will discuss shortly) may not even have a watch or look at a clock. His time passes with the sunrise and sunset. Contrast him with someone working in a corporate job (Orange), reporting to work at a specific time and tightly scheduled in 30-minute increments throughout the day. She's much more conscious of time and perceives it very differently than Beige does.

In summary

The chaos and dissonance we're experiencing is a sign of transformation happening—both societies and individuals advance from layer to layer, in predictable ways. The layer we're in determines how we think, and we have some of each layer within ourselves, like a Russian doll. External factors like life circumstances and the social environment affect how we move between layers. In the next chapter, we'll start to explore exactly what's going on in each of the layers and why some people advance so quickly.

CHAPTER 3

The Colors of Change

Never assume that you are stuck with the way things are.
Life changes every single moment, and so can you.
~RALPH MARSTON

Beck and Cowan assigned colors to the various layers to make them easier to understand and navigate. And when Beck was advising Nelson Mandela in South Africa, the colors were helpful. He could tell Mandela to give his "blue speech" or his "red speech" depending on the audience, so that Mandela shared his consistent message in way that was relevant to each group.

Overall, the warm colors (Beige, Red, Orange, and Yellow) are more "individualistic" and express a "me" focus, and cool colors (Purple, Blue, Green and Turquoise) are more of a "group," "communal" or "we" focus.

Some may criticize The Change Code's layers as being hierarchical. It's worth noting however, that hierarchies occur in nature. The Change Code is a naturally occurring hierarchy, and not an imposed, dominating hierarchy, like the caste system in India. It's similar to other taxonomies we use in science and life so we can understand each other and how things work. In biology, for example, we use taxonomies (e.g., genus, species) to group organisms based on their similarities, and in chemistry, we rely on the periodic table to understand the basic elements of our universe.

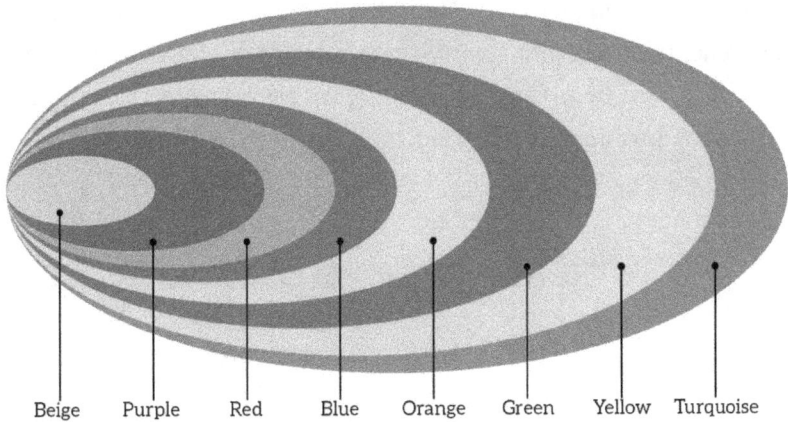

Beige Purple Red Blue Orange Green Yellow Turquoise

Taxonomies are simply a way of meaningfully categorizing nature and life. The Change Code does the same thing based on world views and behaviors (why we think what we think), so we can understand and even predict how to best to live together.

While our similarities are plentiful across all the layers, it's often human nature to default our focus to differences rather than similarities. People in specific layers of the spiral naturally identify with others who share their current layers, often judging and fearing those in surrounding layers, making it difficult to communicate or cooperate —and resulting in polarization.

People often ask if the colors are related to the chakra colors, representing the energy centers of the body. According to Beck, the chakras were not a factor in creating the color system; it was an easy way to distinguish the layers quickly. However, many individuals who apply Graves' theory argue that there is a correlation. This is an area that could be explored by future research.

Though made up of people in multiple colors, societies have one or two dominant colors, and nobody is ever simply at one layer. You may remember from Chapter 2 that we have 13 "streams" of development. These streams include emotional, kinesthetic, morality, creativity, aesthetics, gender, sexuality, empathy, relational, cognitive, spiritual, contemplative, and political. Individuals may be at different layers in these areas, however one color will be dominant across most streams.

The diagram below shows how these various aspects of our development may progress at different rates through the layers.

STREAMS OF DEVELOPMENT

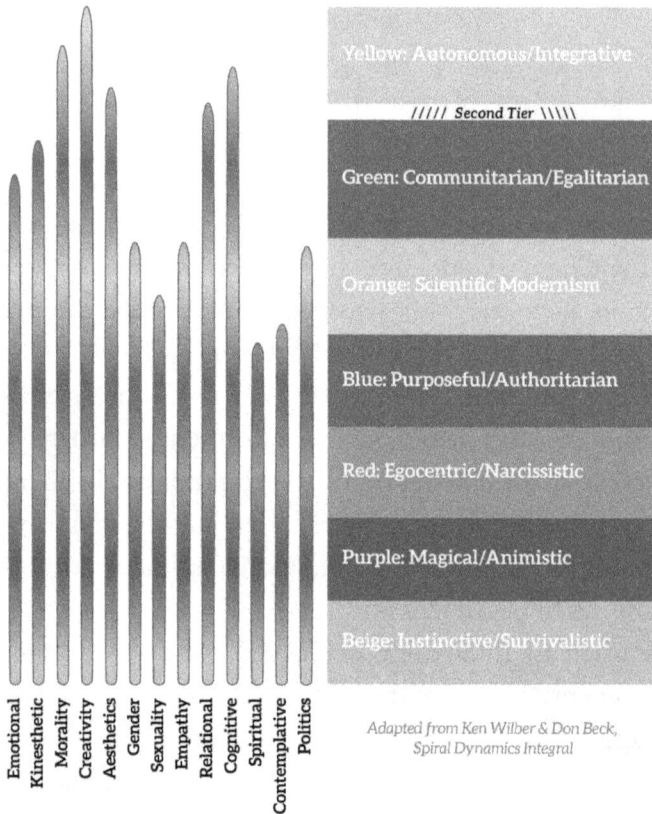

Adapted from Ken Wilber & Don Beck,
Spiral Dynamics Integral

The layers start at Beige and move between left brain/individually focused and right brain/communally focused, creating an upward spiral pattern for human development. Once we reach the yellow layer, we move into the Second Tier where both sides of the brain are activated. The following diagram shows the layers of development. The graphic also shows how we move from less complex to more complex life conditions.

STAGES OF DEVELOPMENT

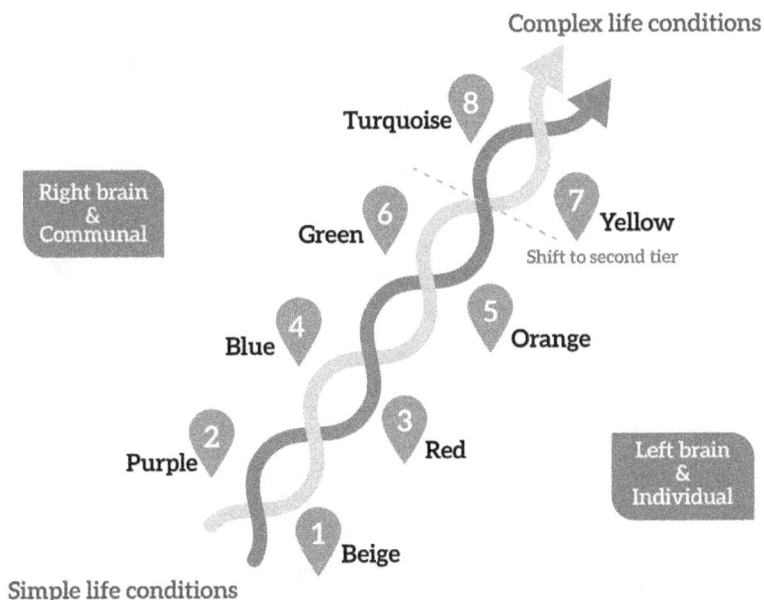

Complex life conditions

Turquoise 8

Right brain & Communal

Green 6

7 Yellow
Shift to second tier

Blue 4

5 Orange

Purple 2

3 Red

Left brain & Individual

1 Beige

Simple life conditions

Adapted from the works of Graves, Beck & Cowan & McDonald
www.thechangecode.net

Before I go into detail with the colors, it's important to remember that these are value systems *within* people; they don't refer to *types* of people. You can't say, for instance, that people who voted for a certain candidate are all a certain color.

Here's a brief overview of each layer:

Beige: Focus is on basic human needs including food, comfort, sleep, reproduction, and safety. There is a limited concept of time, distance, connection, or self-awareness.

Purple: Focus is on family, keeping the good and bad spirits happy and the nest warm and safe. (The first communal layer.)

Red: Focus is on action and assertiveness. Sees the world as a dangerous jungle full of threats and survives by taking from and dominating those who are weaker.

Blue: Focus is on "righteous order," such as church hierarchy or authoritarian government, which enforces a black and white code of conduct, "right" and "wrong," and provides meaning for life.

Orange: Focus is on materialism, driven by technology, scientific advances and competing to win. Individual, success-driven, and sees *many* right paths (unlike Blue).

Green: Focus is on healing the self and the planet, equality and creating networks. Values consensus decisions rather than authority, and seeks harmony.

Yellow: Focus is on personal freedom, but without harm to others or excessive self-interest. Demands open systems, functionality, competence, flow, flexibility, and spontaneity. (The first "integral" layer, incorporating both the right and left sides of the brain.)

Turquoise: Focus is on the power of the universe and the good of all living things (not just humans) as integrated systems. Capable and spiritually oriented, appreciates awe, reverence, gratitude, unity, and simplicity.

OK, so now you understand the basic qualities in each of layers. Next, we'll dive a little deeper into the layers so you can better understand the different world views. This is where it gets really interesting—and *this* is what's going to help connect our polarized world.

Pre-Rational Layers

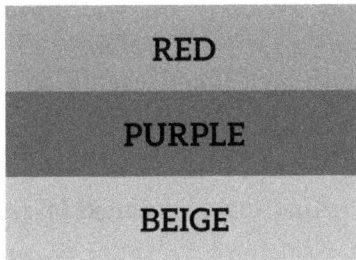

The pre-rational phase, obviously, comes before the dominance of rational thought, and includes the Beige, Purple, and Red layers. People operating from these layers are driven by physical urges and emotions rather than rational decision-making. The pre-frontal cortex has not been fully activated yet.

—

Beige "Instinctive/Survivalistic" (Individual, left-brain focused)

Emerged: 200,000+ years ago

Mantra: *Do what you must to stay alive.*

Core values: Reacting to the environment for survival, but without self-awareness.

This is the starting point for every individual and society. Beige was the stage of the first humans who survived by hunting and gathering. The primary focus is on meeting basic human needs

Beige (Survival)

- *Instinct driven*
- *Hunting/ gathering*
- *Can be very dependent on others*
- *No concept of time, distance*
- *First layer, but may also come from trauma*

including food, comfort, sleep, reproduction, and safety. There is a limited concept of time, distance, connection, or self-awareness.

Beige consciousness can be seen in infants, the homeless, as well as people with mental illness, PTSD, or late-stage Alzheimer's. Individuals may revert to Beige during traumatic events like wildfires, floods, earthquakes, and wars.

Emotion that drives the transition to the next layer: Fear

Transition from Beige to Purple: Humans evolved from beige to purple because they realized there would be more safety in numbers if they worked together. Their life conditions changed when food became harder to find. To survive, humans began to form Tribes and emerged into the next layer: Purple.

—

Purple "Magical/Animistic" (Communal, right brain focused)

Emerged: 50,000 years ago

Mantras: *Keep the spirits happy and the tribe's nest warm and safe.*

Core values: Safety and tradition, ancestors and elders.

Purple began to emerge about 50,000 years ago. This was the first real "we" or communal layer, identifying beyond "me"

Purple (Tribal)

- *Safety-driven*
- *Family*
- *Loyalty*
- *Belonging*
- *Connection*
- *Magical*
- *Rituals*

with the tribe. The basic mode of survival for those perceiving the world through Purple is to keep the good and bad spirits happy and keeping the nest warm and safe.

People operating from the Purple layer seek survival and safety by following the ways of their ancestors, sacrifice, offerings to the gods or spirits, blessings, curses, and spells on their enemies. They honor kinship and lineage, and obedience to the chief and shaman. This is a layer of magical, animistic beliefs: everything has a spirit, rituals, talismans, voodoo.

Purple also seeks harmony with nature and has sacred spaces, objects, and rituals. Individuals perceiving the world through Purple are willing to sacrifice their own wishes for the tribe, the chief, or the spirits.

The Purple layer shows up from ages 1 to 3. Purple is strong in street gangs, athletic teams, and corporate "tribes."

Positive Expressions of Purple: Family and group loyalty.

Negative Expressions of Purple: Superstitions, fear-based living, and a sense of powerlessness.

—

Emotion that drives the transition to the next layer: Anger

Transition from Purple to Red: Individuals and societies begin to transition into Red when the limitations of the tribe became too confining. The rituals and offerings weren't enough to protect the Tribe. The strongest began to take charge and take what they could—they became warriors and conquerors. This is where we see the emergence of extreme egocentrism. Anger also emerges and the pursuit of power and immediate gratification are the primary focus.

—

Red "Egocentric/Narcissistic" (Individual, left-brain focused)

Emerged: 10,000 years ago

Mantra: *Be what you are and do what you want—regardless. Nobody tells me what to do.*

Core Values: Avoiding shame, defending one's reputation, gratifying impulses & senses immediately.

Red (Ego)

- *Power-driven*
- *Taking action*
- *Dominance*
- *Self-centered*
- *World is full of threats*
- *Take what I want*
- *Primal urges*

Red swings back to individualistic consciousness and breaks free of the restraints of the tribe. It comes with a focus on power, and views the world as haves and have-nots, depending on strength or weakness. Red is very egocentric, self-centered, and hedonistic—the self wants to express itself and does not have sufficiently developed perception or emotional capacity to fully understand the impact of its behavior on others.

Here, the world is seen as a dangerous jungle full of threats, and survival comes by aligning with power and taking what you need and dominating those who are weaker. Red is action-oriented and assertive, not analytical or concerned about relationships.

Individuals perceiving the world from through Red will fight one another without any guilt, remorse, or regard for future consequences. Red will do almost anything to avoid shame, defend their reputation, and be respected.

Examples of Red include toddlers going through the "terrible twos," rebellious teens, feudal kingdoms, street gang leaders, soldiers of fortune, and Atilla the Hun.

Positive Expressions of Red: Red energy can be positive when it helps someone lead and take charge in a positive way, say in the athletics arena. Imagine how you've felt when you've started attending a new kind of gym or a workout program.

Negative Expressions of Red: The pitfalls of this layer are anxiety (a fearful world), depression (being oppressed or frustrated by strong competitors), phobias (imagining danger where there is none), and vulnerability to shame.

⌒

Emotion that drives the transition to the next layer: Guilt and shame

Transition from Red to Blue: Red begins to decay when people become tired of the "haves" and "have nots" and enough people get fed up with being pushed around by powerful people and want to impose law and order to benefit everyone. At a deeper level, the individual feels out of control and begins a search for a higher power and a purpose, a right way to live. Blue is a swing back from the "Me" of Red to a tight-knit form of "We," in which the individual makes sacrifices for the benefit of the whole.

Graves described this transition as follows:

> *Ultimately, Red men see that, in spite of their manipulations, life seems not in their control. Egocentric values break down from the weight of the existential problems they create. "What is this all about? Why was I born? Why can't I go on living?" says the 'have.' "Why can't I find some success in life?" asks the miserable 'have not.' Eventually they conclude that life's problems are a sign indicating that if one finds the "right" form of existence the result will be pleasure everlasting." '...the person begins to feel guilty about his or her ensnaring, entrapping, egocentric behavior and begins to say, so to speak, "Well, I'd better sacrifice a little bit of myself to others if I am going to get along in this world."*[26]

⌒

ENTERING First Tier: Rational

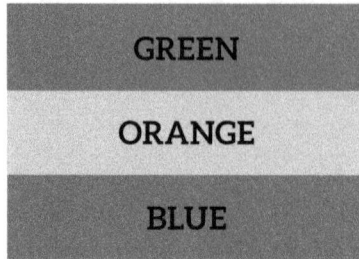

Once we move from Red into Blue, rational thought emerges. Prior to Blue, our thoughts are largely driven by our needs and our emotions. Here we see the more complete activation of the pre-frontal cortex, the area of the brain responsible for decision-making, moderation of instinctive and emotional drivers, social behavior, and complex cognitive behavior. There is a heart opening at Blue that enables the religious "love thy neighbor" capacity and emotionally-driven loyalty between people who are aligned to the same cause (e.g., in marriage, religion, the military, etc.). The rational layers include blue, orange, and green.

———

Blue Layer "Purposeful/Authoritarian" (Communal, Right Brain focused)

Emerged: 5,000 years ago

Mantra: *Life has meaning, direction and purpose determined by a higher order such as a God, religion, or strict political affiliation.*

Core Values: Blue values discipline, duty, regularity, loyalty, and honor. Blue believes in self-sacrifice for later reward (e.g. in heaven) and living according to a strict moral code. Core values include self-discipline, modesty, piety, and morality. There is a focus on good vs. evil. Blue thinking is very linear, absolute, literal, and definite.

Blue is frequently religion-based but can be secular or atheistic. There is always some kind of "righteous order," such as a church hierarchy or authoritarian government, which enforces a black and white code of conduct, teaches "right" and "wrong," and provides meaning for life. Anyone outside the order is wrong and does not deserve respect. The sought-for goal is ultimate peace, often suffering now to receive a reward in the afterlife.

Blue systems are almost always paternalistic, strongly conformist and include rigid social hierarchies, such as the caste system in India. Blue shows up in Puritan America, religious fundamentalism (Christian, Jewish, Islamic), and the Boy Scouts and Girl Scouts.

Blue (Truth)

- *Order-driven*
- *Purposeful life*
- *Stability*
- *Moralistic*
- *Cautious & careful*
- *Tradition*
- *Listens to authority*
- *Only one right way*
- *Rewards to come*
- *Sacrifice for purpose*

In Graves' research, Blue had the highest values for authoritative attitudes and self-control with the lowest values for creating innovations, achieving new concepts, and independence.

Positive Expression of Blue: Blue can bring order and structure, creating the necessary stability for people to live together in large societies.

Negative Expression of Blue: Blue can be negative when it becomes too rigid in role identification, keeping people from developing and changing; script pathology (what you are and do is predetermined); religious fundamentalism; and fascism. Religion is strong for those perceiving the world through Blue, but it is from an "us" vs. "them" perspective. There is only one right way, for example those with a Blue orientation may take a strong stance against other belief systems and even other sects within their own religion (e.g., Sunni vs. Shia, Protestant vs. Catholic, etc.).

Emotion that drives the transition to the next layer: Frustration
Transition from Blue to Orange: Blue begins to decay when individuals see that following the one accepted path doesn't always work. They begin to feel frustrated and confined by the rules and conformity of the group. Orange emerges with a focus on the individual and provides multiple paths to follow, including blazing your own trail. During the transition from Blue to Orange in the United States, we saw the Civil War, which brought the Blue agrarian values of the South into direct conflict with the emerging Orange industrial values of the North.

———

Orange Layer "Scientific Modernism" (Individual, Left-Brain Focused)

Emerged: 300 years ago

Mantra: *Act in your own self-interest by playing the game to win.*

Core values: Independence, success, materialism, technology, and prosperity.

Socially, Orange began about 300 years ago with the Industrial Revolution and the advancement of

Orange (Prosperity)

- *Success driven*
- *Autonomy*
- *Competition*
- *Goal oriented*
- *Leverages influence*
- *Consults experts*
- *High-tech*
- *Image conscious*
- *Wants to prosper now*

science. It's the primary layer in Western society today.

Orange was a swing from the rigid rules and constraints of the Blue layer. When Orange reached a critical mass, the French and American revolutions, the writing of our Constitution, the end of slavery, and the beginning of feminism all happened.

Since Orange emerged, we've seen the development of democracy, put a man on the moon, gone to the depths of the ocean, made tremendous medical advances, and connected the world with technology. We've added an additional 30 years to the average life span during this time and ended most infectious diseases that resulted in mass casualties in the past. We've also seen the end of organized slavery in most developed nations.

This layer is very physically based. It ushers in a rejection of traditional religion and spirituality in favor of modern science. Science began to replace myths, superstitions, and "blind" faith.

Individuals and organizations operating from an Orange perspective are prone to acting in self-interest, playing the game to win. Its valuable contributions are achieving, and measuring success, setting goals and all the modern, labor-saving technology. As a result, the movement from a rural, farm-based economy became an urban, industrialized economy during the Blue/Orange transition.

From the Orange perspective, people begin to question the beliefs and values they have accepted on the authority of parents and teachers, and start to think for themselves. This may lead to rejection of traditional religions, pleasure seeking, and a focus on material world and achievements.

In Graves' data collection, Orange had the highest values for aggression, autonomy, and independence (tied with yellow) with the lowest levels of values for belonging and self-control. Does this sound like anyone you know?

Positive Expressions of Orange: Result-driven, explorative, able to think strategically, pragmatic problem solving, and entrepreneurial.

Negative Expressions of Orange: Identity crisis when traditional values are abandoned, excessive consumerism, manipulative behavior, the environmental crisis, workaholism, loss of connection with nature and each other. Excessive orange leads to a world of winners and losers and the emergence of corporate states. Because Orange is science-based, religion and spirituality are often disregarded or used as tools of manipulation, leaving behind helpful rituals that are beneficial to our overall wellbeing.

Emotion that drives the transition to the next layer: Loneliness

Transition from Orange to Green: Orange begins to break down when overconsumption wreaks havoc and the need for inner peace grows. Here's why: Material success brings the luxury of time to ponder the meaning of life and notice the loneliness and absence of spiritual nourishment. And for most people, burnout from overwork prompts a desire for greater inner peace.

The materialistic nature of this layer no longer meets the needs of an increasingly complex society. Orange took a man to space and connected the world through technology, but from an excessive Orange perspective, humans also feel isolated and alone. Suicide, depression, and drug use increase so the pendulum must swing back to a more communal time to solve these problems, but this time at the higher octave of Green.

———

Green "Communitarian/ Egalitarian" (Communal, Left-Brain Focused)

Emerged: 150 years ago

Mantra: *Seek peace within the inner self and explore, with others, the caring dimensions of community.*

Core values: Connection, communication, sensitivity, cooperation, and networks.

The Green layer began to emerge approximately 150 years ago and

Green (Humanistic)

- *People driven*
- *Heal thyself & the planet*
- *Seeks inner peace*
- *Everyone is equal*
- *Consensus*
- *Politically correct*
- *Social safety nets*
- *Collaborate*
- *Community & networks*
- *Harmony*

swings back to "we" and communal/group awareness. It explores the inner being with a deep sense of community and unity. It tries to share resources equally with all, and to liberate humans from greed and dogma. It values consensus decisions rather than authority and seeks harmony.

An early wave of the Green layer began in the 1960s when Green made up approximately 10 percent of the population in the US. During the 1960s we saw the emergence of "hippies" and the resistance to the Vietnam War. Green also brought the civil rights movement, the environmental movement, and a push for equality of all kinds. In 1962, Rachel Carson published *Silent Spring*, which remains one of the most important, and relatable environmental science books by holding humans (Orange) accountable for abusing our environment with no regard to our or its survival.

Only within the moment of time represented by the present century has one species—man—acquired significant power to alter the nature of the world.

For individuals, this layer may emerge after age 25, although it's important to note that not everyone will move into Green. After age 25, growth or evolution seems to stall, just as physical growth does, unless there is a deliberate effort to push oneself, or the external living conditions somehow push growth.

During the Green layer, network-based systems, such as crypto-currency and block chain technology, have emerged. We've also seen an increase in vegan and vegetarian lifestyles.

In Graves' research, for all layers, Green had the highest values for belonging and the lowest values for independence (tied with Blue).

Positive Expressions of Green include the creation of community, harmony, the acceptance of differences, and compassion for all people and the planet. Green can be very open, warm, empathic, and helpful.

Negative Expressions of Green include conflict avoidance, extreme political correctness, and overly lengthy conversations for consensus and inclusion. Green may also try to impose "Green" solutions in an effort to "help," even when the solution may not be the right one for the situation. Green's need to be liked and included by its peers often gets in the way of independent decision making. Green's challenge is to be able to apply the wisdom of crowds without falling into a sheep mentality of just following the herd.

Presidential candidate and Senator, Elizabeth Warren, recently commented that the news media, politicians, and corporations are distracting Americans with fights over light bulbs and hamburgers. While efforts to personally save energy and reduce water consumption are commendable, Warren points out that these "Green" solutions only address part of our environmental and climate crises, and that we also need to focus on the larger causes.

Some theorists, including Ken Wilber in his book, *Trump and a Post-Truth World*, focus on the negative expressions of Green, calling it the "Mean Green Meme." Wilber talks about Green's culture of narcissism and criticizes its extreme focus on equality resulting in a loss of a shared common truth. Since Green tends to value all opinions, even ill-informed opinions can rise to the surface. Wilber argues that this has led to today's climate of "fake news."

Gravesian theorists believe that humanity will move through the Green layer fairly quickly in response to the urgency of the problems facing us, expanding us to the Second Tier which we will cover next. Since we first became humans at Beige, each successive layer and its associated era has been shorter than the previous one. Green will be successful in establishing new values around human rights, empathy, and sustainability. It sets the foundation for mankind's momentous leap into the Second Tier.

Whole Foods:
Designing a Green Organization to
Serve Green Consumers

If you live anywhere near an American city, you've likely shopped at Whole Foods. Started by John Mackey as a vegetarian grocery store in 1978, the company has grown to more than 500 stores. The profitable company has also made *Fortune's* "100 Best Companies to Work For" every year since the list began.

Whole Foods embodies the Green value system both in the customers it targets—health-conscious consumers who don't mind paying a little more for organic and locally sourced food—but also in its culture and organizational structure. John Mackey talks about the importance of Spiral Dynamics in a keynote speech he gave to employees at their Whole Foods Tribal Gathering in Austin in March of 2006. This talk can be found on the company's blog. Mackey also mentions Spiral Dynamics in his book, *Conscious Capitalism*.

The Green value system is communal and hierarchy avoidant. Green likes to include everyone, collaborate, and work together as a team. It's focused on healing the self and the planet, having a strong mission, and helping others. Sounds like Whole Foods, right?

These values are built into each of the company's systems. Each store has 8-10 teams that help decide what to order, pricing, layout, and perhaps most importantly, who to hire. Once a new employee is hired, they are placed on a team for a trial period. After the trial period, the employee must receive two-thirds majority vote from the team to become an employee. If an employee doesn't receive the necessary votes, they must either find a new team and repeat the process or leave the company. This process is used for employees at all levels of the company and has helped the Whole Foods culture survive through mergers, acquisitions, and periods of rapid growth.

This type of company culture appeals to employees who are within the Green layer. It would likely not appeal to individuals with an Orange-dominant lens because it is very communal, and Orange prefers an individual success-driven and materialistic focus. It would also likely not appeal to individuals with a Red-dominant value system who value strength and dominance in leaders.[27]

The growing influence of Green consumers grew the value of the Whole Foods, as reflected in the recent sale of the company to Amazon for $13.7 billion in 2017.[28] However, since its acquisition by Amazon, Whole Foods has already cut health benefits for part-time employees, reflecting Amazon's Orange-dominant value system. It will be interesting to see if Green consumers continue to support the store if Amazon's culture begins to affect the overall shopping experience.

Emotion that drives the transition to the next layer: Confusion and chaos

Transition from Green to Yellow: At Green, our metaphorical glass becomes full, of thoughts, feelings and responsibilities. We eventually become overloaded with compounding issues of survival, family, power, duty, success and dealing with our (now quite extensive) network of relationships.[29]

The same thing happens to humanity at a global scale—we become overwhelmed by all these compounding issues and the very survival of our species—hence the emergence of groups like "Extinction Rebellion." According to their website, Extinction Rebellion is "an international movement that uses non-violent civil disobedience in an attempt to halt mass extinction and minimize the risk of social collapse."[30]

There are protests and disruptions happening all around us today. Movements for the Climate, Black Lives Matter, Me Too, the Hong Kong rebellion, the Women's March, political protests, human and animal rights protests, and more. The list could go on and on. In its push for human rights and equality, Green is using ongoing protest and chaos to amp up the tension that will inevitably drive change.

Clare Graves put it like this:

Picture, if you will, a Green man seated in a yoga position, contemplating his inner self. He has completed the last theme of the subsistence movement of existence. There are no new deficiency motivations to rouse him from his meditations.

In fact, he might well go on to contemplating his navel to the day of his death, if he only had some suitable arrangement to care for his daily needs. And it is quite possible for a few Green individuals to live this way.

But what happens when the majority of a population begins to arrive at the Green level of existence? Who is left to care for their daily needs? Who is left to look after the elaborate technology which assures their survival? If we return to Green man seated in his yoga position, we see that what finally disturbs him is the roof falling in on his head.[31]

Eventually, as Graves said the roof falls in on our head and the resulting chaos creates the necessary evolutionary tension for our transformation to Yellow. At Yellow, we become disentangled from the first-tier systems, freeing up considerable emotional and psychological space, which leads to a quantum leap in our coping capacity.

This emotional freedom at Yellow is sometimes misinterpreted as coldness, however this is a misunderstanding. The information and knowledge that becomes available to us at Yellow radically transforms our perspective and our behavior. The following allegory or "nyaya" from the Vedanta school of Hindu philosophy explains it better than I can.[32]

In the twilight a man treads upon a rope, and mistaking it for a poisonous snake, jumps in hurry, and cries out in fear. His heart throbs quickly. But when a light is brought by a friend of his, he finds that it is not a snake but only a rope, and then all his fears vanish.

The Yellow perspective is like the light in this allegory. What was previously hidden to us in the first six layers is now revealed and our fears dissolve. Because we live in such a fearful world, a person who is fearless and not emotionally reactive might be seen as cold. They are also better able to cope and solve the complex problems created in the first six layers.

Beyond the Rational/Second Tier

> ### TURQUOISE
>
> ### YELLOW

Graves called the layers after Green the "Second Tier" because they begin to repeat the earlier layers' themes, but they're more advanced. As Graves compared the layers to a symphony, these next layers are at a higher octave.

At this stage, we still have access to the rational mind, but are now able to access new dimensions including a deep intuition. One of the biggest indicators of the shift into the Second Tier is the absence of fear as a driver of behavior. No longer driven by fear, we live in a state of flow with nature. And we overcome other compulsive behaviors that are so prominent in the earlier levels.

Being comfortable with paradox in general opens up a whole new world of possibility, and according to Graves, the Second Tier has more coping capacity (ability to understand and cope with complexity) than all previous layers combined. This is huge!

Here's a way to think about it. An interesting expression of comfort-with-paradox is reflected in the current increase in gender fluidity in Generation Z (born mid-1990s to early 2000s). According to Nadya Okamoto, the 21-year old co-founder of Period.org, a non-profit providing sanitary supplies to the homeless, and Juve Media, a consulting firm for brands wanting to reach this generation, Gen Z has two nicknames. "Plurals," because they think in terms of "we," and "the genderless generation," because fewer than 50 percent of them identify as completely heterosexual and reject the idea of gender binaries like male/female.[33]

I'm not aware of any societies in Yellow (yet) but there are some Scandinavian countries that are well into Green and beginning to move toward Yellow. There are many people already in Yellow and Turquoise, with more moving into these layers every day. We can expect that as more people move into these layers, a tipping point will be reached.

Second Tier allows us to meet people where they are. This also makes it difficult to spot other people on Second Tier—they are shape-shifters. They easily relate and fit in with others who think they are one of their tribe, without hurting or excluding others. This ability to relate extends to people with opposing political opinions, financial backgrounds, race, etc. They find common ground between diverse individuals and create win-win solutions. Does this describe anyone you know?

Graves' work helps us understand that our current conditions and chaos are temporary. We are in the midst of a major transition and there is hope. If we can just make it through Green to Yellow...

We will find ourselves in a very different world from what we know now and we will find ourselves thinking in a very different way. For one thing, we will no longer be living in a world of unbridled self-expression and self-indulgence or in a world of reverence for the individual, but in one whose rule is: Express self, but only so that all life can continue....

The purpose of Yellow man will be to bring the earth back to equilibrium so that life upon it can survive, and this involves learning to act within the limits inherent in the balance of life. We may find such vital human concerns as food and procreation falling under strict regulation, while in other respects society will be free not only from any form of compulsion but also from prejudice and bigotry....

While more naturalistic than the world we know today, at the same time the Second-Tier world will be unimaginably more advanced technologically; for unlike Green man, Yellow man will have no fear of technology and will understand its consequences. He will truly know when to use it and when not to use it, rather than being bent on using it whenever possible as Orange man has done.[34]

In 2018, Ken Wilber wrote that only about 5 percent of the total population "is at any of these integral stages of development, but the evidence is that this is clearly where tomorrow's evolution eventually will go—if it can survive the present transition."[35]

Yellow "Autonomous/Integrative" (Individual/Integrated Brain)

Emerged: 100 years ago

Mantra: *Flexibility and natural flows.*

Core values: Knowledge and cosmic reality, using the best evidence possible, regardless of where it comes from (an openness to all theories, models, religions, etc.)

Yellow (Flow)

- *Process-driven*
- *Living in flow*
- *Integral (both sides of brain)*
- *Principled*
- *Competency*
- *Acceptance of change & chaos*
- *Big picture views*

The Yellow layer has begun to emerge and is our first leap into the Second Tier. It began about 50 years ago, in the 1960s, just 100 years after the onset of Green.

Just as Beige was the first baby step into being human, Yellow is the first baby step into a whole new realm of a multidimensional existence.

This layer again swings away from communal to individual, but with a difference. Individuals perceiving the world through the Yellow layer are able to accept a mix of conflicting "truths" and uncertainties. They value personal freedom but without harm to others or excess self-interest. Yellow demands open systems. The focus is on functionality, competence, flexibility, and spontaneity. It opens up our sensory perceptions in a new way.

This layer is also called the Integral Level because we are able to effectively work with, or integrate, both sides of our brain. Without constant fear, anxiety, and compulsions, we have more psychological energy than previous layers and can allocate it to solving complex problems that didn't previously seem to have solutions.

In Graves' research, for all layers, Yellow had the highest values for creating innovations and autonomy (tied with Orange) with the lowest values for an authoritative attitude.

Yellow is the first layer that can directly sense the active value systems in other people—like a frequency being transmitted. This gives access to an entirely new way of relating with other human beings. When you can read a person's worldview and immediately know their challenges and motivations, without any feelings of rejection, you more deeply understand and interact with that person.

Positive Expressions of Yellow: curiosity without judging and the ability to ask the right questions. Yellow is creative and innovative and has a continuous flow of new ideas and ways of thinking. Yellow uses the most appropriate and workable methods and behaviors to realize strategies and builds on already existing knowledge and models. Individuals in the Yellow layer are able to better meet others where they are now.

Negative Expressions of Yellow: In the game-changing Second Tier, there are few, if any, negative expressions because there's no fear, rejection, or compulsive behaviors.

—

Transition from Yellow to Turquoise: Yellow begins to break down when the new form of individualism fails to yield the kind of cooperation necessary for humanity's survival. Turquoise emerges.

—

**Turquoise
"Holistic" (Communal/
Integrated Brain)**

Emerged: 30 years ago

Mantra: *Experience the wholeness of existence through mind and spirit.*

Core Values: Experiential spirituality, minimalism, awe, unity, simplicity, poetic perception of reality, action through inaction.

Turquoise (Holistic)

- *Synthesis driven*
- *Global view*
- *Renewal*
- *Spiritual*
- *Awe, gratitude, unity*
- *Simplicity*
- *Honors all living things*

Turquoise is still taking shape and only makes up a small part of the population. It began about 30 years ago in the 1990s (just 20 years after Yellow!). The Turquoise layer is a collective blend of individuals who insist on a trusting and respectful environment.

Individuals operating from Turquoise are very capable and spiritually oriented, with their spirituality resembling panentheism more than more dogmatic and patriarchal religions of our time.[36]

They have an appreciation for awe, reverence, gratitude, unity, and simplicity. They feel connected to the power of the universe and focus on the good of all living things (not just humans) as integrated systems. There is an expanded use of brain/mind tools and global networking and connection is the norm. This is likely the first layer that will be able to bring true global stability.

Turquoise detects holistic energy flows that bind everything together and identifies solutions to protect all life.

Turquoise is a repeat of Purple themes, only at a higher octave and more complexity, but now the tribe is the entire planet and possibly beyond. Just *one* individual operating from the Turquoise layer can make a tremendous contribution to the planet.

Graves characterized Turquoise in a 1970 paper.

Through personal experience, these individuals show that—no matter how much information is available—not everything can be understood. Astonishment, awe, reverence, gratitude, unity and simplicity are appreciated. Reality can be experienced, but one can never be certain about it.

There is an atmosphere of trust and respect. They stand up against constraints and limitations on a quiet and personal manner—never in a showcasing manner. They avoid relationships in which others try to dominate—do not like to dominate others but rather specify a clear direction insofar as it is necessary.[37]

Positive expressions of Turquoise: To see the world and the cosmos as an integral whole. To explore, feel and pragmatically work together to solve the large complex problems to serve humanity and the earth. Turquoise has an uncanny ability to capture truth, knowledge, and diverse perspectives for integration into their systems. Turquoise is energetically in tune with the Universe. They are compassionate, but at the same time, can clearly see and do what needs to be done.

Next Layers

Because Graves' model has no end, there are layers beyond Turquoise. Beck and Cowan claim that a Coral layer exists but haven't been able to identify enough people in this layer yet to make it statistically significant.

Ken Wilber also believes the Coral layer exists—and more layers beyond that. He calls the layer after Turquoise (which would include Coral) the "Third Tier" of consciousness and says that fully realized beings such as Jesus and Buddha likely evolved to this Third Tier. Unitive consciousness and universal love and compassion characterize this layer.[38]

Find additional information on the layers in the Appendix.

Role-Playing Colors

Tony Robbins, personal development author and speaker, has used this theory at his Date with Destiny retreats. He teaches the various layers and then assigns the audience to role-play specific colors. Tony asks people from each color what they think of other colors. Red may have a hard time understanding how anyone could think like Green (fights have even broken out as Reds are all about control, power, and domination), and Orange tends to use any piece of information to their advantage. Participants gain insight into why people do the things they do. It's an interesting exercise that you can also try with a partner. Take turns having conversations from each color's perspective.[39]

How to Move Between Layers

I'm frequently asked how to move from one layer to the next and how to help others move. Just a reminder: we cannot say that one layer is "better" than another. Each layer is based on life conditions. The best layer for a person or society is the one that is most *aligned* with existing life conditions. When a layer stops functioning in the current life conditions, a move to the next layer is beneficial. You can't simply "will yourself" to the next layer or force other people to change.

On the other hand, it is beneficial to create positive life conditions in a community to support the healthy development of individuals and society as a whole. As Graves said:

For the overall welfare of total man's existence in this world, over the long run of time, higher levels are better than lower levels and the prime good of any society's governing figures should be to promote human movement up the levels of human existence.

Changing layers is not an easy process. It happens, usually gradually, in response to life conditions and/or because of our own inner work and growth. While life experiences can naturally move us along, most of us must also commit to working toward change, especially when advancing to, and through, the Second Tier.

Tension is the key factor for moving from one layer to the next. There has to be enough tension in your life conditions to create discomfort. This discomfort is so strong that you know things can't stay the same, you have to change and find new ways for coping with the world. The earlier you can recognize this tension and act on it, the better.

Practices involving altered states can be effective in expediting the movement from one layer to another. These practices have been used since the dawn of time for self-exploration, insights, and personal development. The structured use of altered states was all but lost from Western civilization. However, a renaissance is underway thanks to influence from Eastern cultures.[40]

Ken Wilber has said that a consistent meditation practice is an important part of a Second-Tier lifestyle. And this makes sense: as we grow with our meditation practice, we are better able to tap into intuition, release negative feelings and emotions, and maintain a calm inner state that makes us more available to transformation. I'll get into meditation more in Chapter 6.

Your Colors

Did you recognize yourself in any of the color descriptions? I've created a free assessment that you can take to find out your colors. This assessment is available on our website at www.TheChangeCode.net. You will receive a report with the results of your assessment, showing you a ranking of your top value systems by color.

In summary

Our American society is, for the most part, in the first tier, with most people at the Orange or Green layers. While entire societies have not reached the Second-Tier Yellow layer, many individuals have.

Much of the polarization we're seeing in the world has to do with the shifting of consciousness to a new layer, and the clash in values that results. The transition from one layer to the next is not necessarily smooth. No layer is good or bad---each has positive and negative expressions. And the model doesn't end, as long as there is evolution, there will be more layers.

Now, we'll look at what's happening in the U.S. today, why it's so uncomfortable, and find some signs of hope.

CHAPTER 4

A Major Paradigm Shift –
What is Really Happening Here?

The world as we have created it is a process of our thinking.
It cannot be changed without changing our thinking.
~ALBERT EINSTEIN

In the U.S., we have individuals in a greater number of active parallel layers than at any time in human history. This means that as a country, we've got folks in every layer from Beige to Turquoise. These value systems run parallel as people with very different world views work together, live on the same streets, and shop at the same stores. From the outside, there is no noticeable difference, but how people think and perceive what is happening around them can be quite different.

The U.S. has been primarily dominated by the Orange worldview since the Industrial Revolution, focused on science, materialism, individuality, and success. None of these traits are bad, except when they become extreme, which is what we are seeing today. It's prompting the shift to Green.

Green first began to appear in the mid 1800s with social justice movements. These became a significant wave in the 1960s. Remember, Green values community, healing the self and caring for the planet, deep connection, and a leveling of the hierarchies. Today, we're at a tipping point and undergoing a paradigm shift—enough people have moved into the Green layer or higher, to begin the shift beyond the Orange-dominant worldview. This is the same type of shift that happened during the Industrial Revolution, but at a higher octave.

The result: feelings of chaos. The systems established during the Orange layer are losing their effectiveness and appear in many cases to be falling apart. Think of what's going on in our schools, our government, our religious institutions, and our healthcare and economic systems. Our society and the individuals within it have become more complex, and our systems aren't keeping pace. This is what is leading to the feeling that "things just aren't working."

In times of uncertainty, we seek out comfort. History has shown us that we also lean toward authoritarian leadership. This is a regression to earlier value sets, in this case, Blue. We are seeing this regression in many parts of the world today, including in the U.S.

At the same time, a small number of people are moving into the Yellow layer. You may remember, Yellow is the first layer in the "Second Tier" of consciousness, a tremendous leap for humankind. Individuals perceiving the world from the Yellow layer let go of irrational fears and anxiety, have integrated the right and left sides of the brain, and are no longer limited to absolute truths. They understand complexities and integrate many different perspectives to identify innovative solutions. Individuals in these layers have very different operating systems, values, and views of the world, which are based on their life conditions.

The differences between so many active layers cause an ongoing friction like the earth's tectonic plates rubbing together. When the friction gets so high, there's general unrest, riots, and maybe even war.

You'll remember in Chapter 2, we discussed how change really happens, and that before an individual or society moves to the next layer, they tend to regress in an attempt to recreate harmony in their world. We are currently witnessing a regression from the Orange layer to the Blue layer. Think about sayings like "the good old days" and "Make America Great Again." These are the desires expressed by people wanting to go back to a simpler time.

My friend Anita is socially and environmentally conscious and works to reduce her impact on the environment (Green). However, when she was fired from her job last year and feeling a tremendous amount of stress, she indulged in a huge shopping spree, buying clothes and shoes she didn't need in an effort to feel better. Ten years ago, shopping was relaxing for her. Not so much anymore. She admits she fell back into egocentric Red behavior as a result of the stress.

It's also natural for humans to fear the next layer. It's because the new layer calls into question our core beliefs about ourselves, the world, and our place in the world. We also reject previous layers, even though there are positives in each one, because we feel like we've moved beyond that way of being.

It's like that rubber band being pulled back; more dramatic tension is actually the impetus for change. As much as we would like to avoid change, the coping mechanisms that were effective in earlier layers no longer work. When it becomes clear that what we're doing is no longer working, we reach the sometimes harsh conclusion that change will be necessary for survival.

You are likely seeing this all around you. Picture a businessman who has made his life and his fortune by selling coal. He becomes fearful about how he will continue to accumulate wealth if we move from coal to cleaner alternatives (a Green value). So, to protect himself, he fights clean-energy legislation even as there is mounting evidence about the damage coal causes to the environment. This fear causes a backlash against Green, and his employees, the coal miners, join in the resistance to change. While they haven't grown rich from coal mining, it's part of their families' heritage and histories, and they fear how they'll survive if the coal industry disappears. This is an example of people coming together to resist a societal shift to move past Orange.

The Orange system provided invaluable technological and medical advancements for humanity through the use of science. Orange developed computers that now allows us to communicate with anyone in the world in real-time. (Creating the Internet is a Green value.) But Orange also developed nuclear bombs and weapons of mass destruction. The

Orange layer is individual or "me" focused, without much empathy. Our Orange materialism has filled our oceans with discarded plastic and put our planet in peril.

However, as with every layer we move through as a society, eventually the pendulum swings too far, which causes problems that can only be solved by a paradigm shift. That happens when the *Me* versus *We* pendulum swings back the other way and society moves to the next layer.

Go to Costco on a beautiful summer afternoon, and you'll see plenty of evidence that the Orange layer of materialism is still deeply ingrained in our society. Hundreds of people piling unnecessary amounts of food, clothing, and housewares into their carts, spending money they don't have for things they likely don't need. Hey, I've been there too, and when I see a good sale, my Orange layer still comes out.

Although the Orange value system helped us solve many existing problems in society, including the rigidity of the Blue layer, the pendulum has again swung too far. Continuing the current trajectory is not sustainable.

Among other things, the result of too much materialism and individualism has been high rates of depression, suicide, and drug abuse. People feel more disconnected than ever before and our extreme materialism has put our planet in turmoil with melting glaciers, extreme weather, out-of-control plastic consuming our oceans and landfills, deforestation, and unfortunate loss of animal, plant, and insect species.

In *The Second Mountain*, David Brooks refers to the Four "Interrelated Social Crises" that result from this extreme individualism. These are:

1. *The Loneliness Crisis:*

More than 35% of Americans over 45 are chronically lonely and we've stopped talking to our neighbors. Only 8% of Americans report having important conversations with their neighbors in a given year. The psychological, social, and moral toll caused by this detachment is horrific. Since 1999, the US suicide rate has risen by 30% to roughly 45,000 suicides per year. Opioids kill another 72,000

American per year. These are known as "deaths of despair," resulting in the first decrease in the average life span since 1918.

2.   *The Distrust Crisis:*
Our culture has moved into a permanent state of distrust. It seems like everyone is just out for themselves, and they are. "Distrust breeds distrust. When people feel distrustful, they conclude that the only person they can rely on is themselves."

3.   *The Meaning Crisis:*
There is a pervasive "lack of meaning" in our society and related mental health problems such as depression and suicide are seeing a significant increase.

4.   *The Tribalism Crisis:*
"Individualism, taken too far, leads to tribalism." Those who are feeling disconnected look for a way to return to the bonds of community, unfortunately tribalism provides the dark side of community. Instead of community based on mutual affection, tribalism provides connection based on mutual hatred.

"True loneliness, Nabeelah Jaffer writes, is not only solitude; it is also a sort of spiritual emptiness, the loss of faith in oneself to come up with answers, 'the loss of one's own self'." Jaffer points out that this loneliness is what prompts many to join extremists' groups, including the Islamic State, to find a sense of belonging.[41]

As a society, when we moved from order-driven and moralistic Blue, to the scientific, materialistic Orange, there was a rejection of Blue values. You'll remember the rejection of the earlier value system is human nature and is part of development until we reach Second Tier (Yellow, Turquoise).

With the rejection of Blue values, though, we moved away from religion in many parts of the world in favor of Science. As a result, we've seen an increase in atheism and materialism, especially among science-minded people. Materialists believe the universe is unconscious; made up of mindless matter; and governed by impersonal, mathematical laws.

A popular new group of atheists, like author/podcaster/neuroscientist Sam Harris, and scientist Richard Dawkins have developed an enormous following among people who are seeking meaning in life without religion. They believe religion causes more harm than good and that humans have moved beyond it.

This viewpoint and others has led to a decline in traditional religious observances. Europe has often been referred to as post-Christian— even though it's home to the world's most spectacular churches and cathedrals. Only a small percentage of European's practice Christianity on a regular basis. In the United States more people say they believe in God, but only 36 percent of the population attends church regularly.[42]

The rejection of religion has also resulted in the loss of the religious community—where people come together weekly, feel connected, sing, and practice sacred rituals. This loss has only increased the feelings of isolation.

Let me explain this another way. As Orange values replaced Blue values, people disconnected from traditional religion, nature, and the environment, and technology replaced human connection. We became more and more individualistic, which allowed us to achieve many things. As we welcomed space travel, computers, and weapons of mass destruction, we also lost beautiful things like ritual, community, and sharing sorrows and celebrations. Even weddings, which used to be important family and community gatherings, are decreasing as more marriage-aged millennials wait to get married, choose the single life, or just avoid the pomp and circumstance of a ceremony.

Now with the dominant paradigm at late-stage Orange, the shift has gone too far, and we are experiencing far more isolation and loneliness than ever before. But nature is stepping in and our society is auto-correcting. The pendulum is beginning to swing back and up to a more communal way of living (Green).

Fascinating, right? Think of how many young people are actually giving up technology and going back to the land, knitting, and growing their own food and animals. After many generations, there's a resurgence in homesteading and a movement from the city to the country in search of a simpler lifestyle.

From Orange to Green

The table below summarizes some of the changes that come with this shift:

Orange	Green
Individually Focused	Communal Focused, Connection with others
Left Brain	Right Brain
Competition	Collaboration
Short-term gains	Long-term sustainability
Disconnected with nature	Reconnect with nature
Conquering the planet	Healing the planet
Controlling the self, including emotions	Healing the self, personal growth
Focus on science & technology	Focus on intuition, connection, spirituality
Autonomy	Network, Inclusion
Winners and Losers	Equality
Paternalistic	Maternalism
Sympathy	Empathy

Signs of Green are everywhere, as more and more businesses recognize the importance of sustainable and conscious services and products, naturopathic medicine, coaching and self-help groups, and vegetarianism and veganism have become mainstream. Consumer demand is shaping the marketplace.

Sixty six percent of consumers would spend more on a product if it came from a sustainable brand. Up to 73% of the surveyed millennials had a similar view. And according to Horizon Media's Finger on the Pulse study, 81% of millennials expect companies to declare their corporate citizenship publicly.[43]

As we make this shift, here's what to look for. You'll remember that it's human nature to reject elements of the previous layer. We see this already with calls to end capitalism and a backlash against science by a growing number of science-deniers. And while Orange has created major problems on the planet with its excessive materialism and extreme individualism, we are going to need aspects of Orange to help solve these problems. We don't want to throw it out completely.

One example is the use of artificial intelligence to help save the rare snow leopard. Biologists suspect we are witnessing the sixth mass extinction on the planet today,[44] and the snow leopard is one species that we're on the verge of losing. Microsoft is now applying artificial intelligence (AI) technology to help scientists study and hopefully save the snow leopard. The Snow Leopard Trust uses this technology in their trail cams to watch for snow leopards, which are incredibly hard to spot. The AI helps identify the snow leopards quickly, making their research more effective.[45]

Next, we also need to be aware of negative expressions of Green (and all layers) and potential unintended consequences. The Green backlash against science (Orange) has the unintended consequence of skewing research with too much "crowd sourcing." For example, Green says, "97 percent of scientists agree that we have global warming, therefore it must be correct." Due to Green's desire to collapse hierarchies of all kinds, it also tends to overlook cause-and-effect relationships that result from hierarchies, including those used in science.

While the majority of scientists agree that our climate is changing and that humans are a major contributing factor, there are diverse views about what that means, the ultimate outcome, and the specific causes. Some scientists such as Professor Valentina Zharkova, a mathematician and astrophysicist from Northumbria University, are finding indicators for global cooling, which could potentially result in the next mini ice age. Her radically different (although not unique) perspective emerged from her study of the sun's internal energy flows and their influence on the earth. These factors could significantly impact our climate, but are disregarded by most scientists.

The real truth is probably somewhere in between. Only by taking a complex-systems approach to reviewing and understanding the research will we be able to come up with solid conclusions.

Green has also introduced a moral imperative to science which is driven by fear, especially in the case of climate science. If you don't agree with Green's crowd-sourced opinion, then you don't just disagree, your moral character is flawed.

Another example of unintentional consequences from Green is the rewriting of history books to be more inclusive, accurate, and culturally sensitive. While the intentions are good, there have been unintended consequences. Take the backlash against Christopher Columbus and his actions related to the European discovery of America. Some states, including Vermont, Maine, New Mexico, Alaska, North Carolina, and South Dakota are replacing Columbus Day as a holiday with Indigenous People's Day.[46]

While there are good reasons for revising this story, it's been a centerpiece to the identity of America and who we are as a nation. When we extricate parts of our identity without filling those voids, there is pushback, confusion, and feelings of loss. We need to acknowledge this loss, and help create a new narrative. We need to develop a new story as a nation, one that we can share and have pride in. We'll discuss this more in Chapter 8.

In summary

Our society, and much of the world, is in the midst of a major paradigm shift.

It's natural to fear the shift, because it can call into question our core beliefs. Moving from Blue to Orange and its extreme individualism, we lost many good things: community, sacred rituals, and singing together. But as we move from Orange to Green as a society, we can choose to use positive aspects of Orange (i.e., technology and science) to help solve problems in a new way, rather than rejecting that layer altogether.

As Agents for Change, we can help others understand what's happening, reduce chaos, and help create a brighter future. We'll discuss how in the next chapter.

CHAPTER 5

Easing the Transition and Designing the Future

You never change things by fighting against the existing reality.
To change something, build a new model that makes the old model obsolete.
~BUCKMINSTER FULLER

While it's tempting to get caught up in the polarization and drama of our time, as a leader and a visionary, your role is not to fight what is, but to *design the future.*

If you're reading this book, you're looking for solutions.

Any layer can make a positive impact, but those viewing the world from a Green or Yellow perspective may feel an urgency to help society ease tensions during the transition we're going through. And many of us are highly-sensitive and empathic, deeply feeling the emotions of others. This gives us even more to process. These strong emotions and the reactions of others may leave us feeling out of place, unsure what to do, and uncertain where we belong.

Graves teaches us that life conditions are the key for human change and evolution. As life conditions become more complex, we adapt to survive. Well, I think we can agree, the complex life conditions are here and all around us. But what *do* we do and *where* do we go next?

Letting Go

For our world to transform we must let go of what is crumbling—gracefully. By definition, our existing systems were all created under Blue and Orange layers to meet the needs of the day. Everyone did the best they could to build a society that made sense. Now, many of the institutions created then are hundreds of years old, both the buildings and the operating structures. They've done a good job supporting our society to get to where we are now. But they simply aren't enough to help us get to the next level.

Take, for instance, our Education system. With the exception of technology, many schools are teaching nearly the same curriculum in nearly the same way they were 50 or 100 years ago. Maybe reading, writing, and arithmetic were enough then—but what about understanding complex systems, collaboratively leading change, emotional intelligence, and how to develop as a human?

As much as we may want to go back to a simpler time, or to make everything "great" again, it doesn't work that way. There is no standing still, no going back. In life, if you're not growing and evolving, you're dying. For humans to survive, we will need to grow and evolve.

The Lakota Indians understand this principle well. They use the term, *skan*, which means "movement exists." As long as we are alive, everything will be constantly moving and changing, that's the nature of life. Change is inevitable. It only becomes a problem when we attach judgement to it and label a change as bad or wrong. When we recognize change as a natural part of life, the process becomes easier.

Increasing Complexity

One transformation currently underway is in our understanding of problem solving and the nature of complex systems. We generally make sense of the world through a relatively simple cause-and-effect lens: "if I do A, then I'll get B." For example, if I put water in my teapot and turn on the heat, it will boil. This is linear thinking, which became dominant during the Blue layer. This leads us to believe we can control the outcome of a situation by taking a specific action.

However, the complexity of our world has increased significantly over the past century. Today, there are more than 7.7 billion people on the planet,[47] more than twice the number that we had just 60 years ago. Humans are using far more resources than ever before and are far more interconnected. And, you'll remember from earlier chapters, we now have people in more color layers at the same time than ever before in human history.

This means people have very different views of how best to solve problems.

Besides, few modern problems have just one cause and one effect— unless you're trying to figure out why your tea water isn't boiling. Problems are typically complex and non-linear: Think depression. Addiction. Climate change. Healthcare.

In *Chaos: Making a New Science*, author James Gleick writes:

Linear relationships are easy to think about: the more the merrier. Linear equations are solvable, which makes them suitable for text-books...you can take them apart and put them together again – the pieces add up.

Nonlinear systems generally cannot be solved and cannot be added together...Nonlinearity means that the act of playing the game has a way of changing the rules...That twisted changeability makes non-linearity hard to calculate, but it also creates rich kinds of behavior that never occur in linear systems.[48]

A complex, non-linear system is a set of things (people, cells, molecules, etc.) that are interconnected in such a way that they produce their own patterns of behavior over time. For instance, an anthill is a biologically complex system. From the outside, an ant hill looks simple, but when you dig down you'll discover a complex skyscraper-like structure built without a blueprint or leader and connected by a network of parallel layers and tunnels.

To a large extent, a complex system causes its own behavior. To make it even more complex, these systems can be nested inside one another.

> "For every complex problem, there is a simple solution. And it's wrong."

Again, stay with me here as I explain.

Many complex systems are also adaptive, such as the human body and our planet's climate. They are adaptive because they attempt to self-regulate in a movement toward homeostasis or equilibrium.

A complex system is more than the sum of its parts, which means you can't understand a complex system just by identifying the parts. Problems within these systems can be difficult to solve because there are often delays in feedback. When a system is also adaptive, outcomes are even less predictable.[49]

There is a well-known saying in the systems arena, "For every complex problem, there is a simple solution. And it's wrong."

Imagine a group of experts coming together to tackle the problem of a salmon die-off in a local river. Instead of offering solutions immediately, they'll ask questions like who uses the river, what water sources feed into it, what water sources the river feeds into, what data sources are available about the river's history, what the native species and non-native species are, and more. They would look at the problem holistically to get to the root causes of the problem.

And they won't rush. Perhaps the most difficult aspect of leading change is not racing to a solution. It takes time and effort to identify the underlying patterns in a complex system. Doing so however, allows us to see what aspects keep the system stable and identify leverage points (places to apply pressure for change).

So, unfortunately, there aren't a lot of quick fixes or silver bullets for the problems we're facing. Leading the change will require patience, new skills, and an understanding of complex systems and systems thinking.

Leading the Change

As society inevitably makes its way further into Green, and then very quickly (some say within 20 years or less) moves into Yellow, leaders need to prepare the systems and framework to ease the transition and ensure success.

The current systems are struggling to stay afloat, and small "tweaks" aren't going to fix them. Going back to the education example, for instance, just adding a few courses is not going to prepare students for the emerging need for a fundamental shift in thinking and problem-solving skills. Today's high school students should be preparing for the jobs of the future, many of which don't exist yet.

> As Dr. Beck puts it, our goal as leaders is to "Thrive, and Help Thrive."

These changes will require *new* systems designed from new ways of thinking. While our existing systems worked for many years, they haven't kept up with our rapidly changing society. As changemakers and visionaries, you're the ones who will see possible solutions and determine which systems need to be replaced. You are the pathfinders that Graves described in his research. I will refer to you as Agents for Change.

Designing the new systems will help change the life conditions for those on the verge of transitioning to the next layer, speeding up the process for them and for society as a whole.

However, the new systems will also need ways to support and engage every layer, because there will always be individuals at every layer. All humans are worthy and have an important role in society. As Dr. Beck puts it, our goal as leaders is to "Thrive, and Help Thrive."

From Social Enterprise to a Systems Change Lens

As a changemaker, you may be an entrepreneur or a budding entrepreneur looking to create a social enterprise. Social entrepreneurs like Richard Branson and Elon Musk have a massive impact on society. I'm a proponent of social entrepreneurship and the whole Conscious Capitalism movement because it has so much potential and it's moving in the right direction.

However, changing outdated and failing systems is going to take more than just a clever new venture. There are a range of interconnected shifts that need to happen. We need to shift our focus from *social enterprise* to a *systems-change* lens.

CHANGE CODE IN ACTION

IN 2007, LILY LAPENNA started MyBnk in the UK to address the lack of financial education among young people. She developed programs for financial literacy to be used within schools and youth groups. After a few years of selling her offerings around the UK, Lily partnered with her competitors to create a bigger impact. She and Young Money created a financial education group that included government officials, financial education providers, and entrepreneurs. Within two years, this group was able to change laws in the UK, something Lily wouldn't have been able to accomplish as easily on her own. As she writes:

If we had been working with social investors who wanted us to simply focus on financial sustainability, they might not have been have happy to see their CEO spending so much time at meetings with competitors or policy makers.

This shift, from building and scaling our social enterprise to contributing to wider systems–level work, was one that took a perspective, mindset, and skill shift. **We might have more people making that shift if all social entrepreneurs who want to contribute to solving social or environmental problems were given training on working with government, influencing policy change, and collaborating across networks.** *Those skills aren't taught in most social enterprise start–up programs, but they should be!*

Lily was named a Member of the Order of the British Empire (MBE) by the Queen for her work, and MyBnk continues to grow both as a social enterprise and as an advocate for wider systems change for youth financial education.[50]

System Design and Transformation

Effective system design is the key to how we will be able to coexist with so many different simultaneous layers in our growingly complex world. The systems needing effective design include our government, education, judicial, healthcare, financial, and more.

Our systems determine how individuals will function within a society and how we will work together.

There is no playbook for designing the systems for the future. It's something each of us will have to do in our own way. And it requires each of us to do our inner work, develop an understanding of complex systems, learn effective change-management skills, and continually refine our leadership abilities. There are some clear themes already emerging in the Orange to Green transition, however. These include:

- Rebuilding local communities and systems.
- Redeveloping local supply systems, especially organic food.
- Decentralizing systems from global networks to bring more local control.
- Focusing on the customer experience and not just making a profit.

Over time, we can expect to see more of Yellow's influence on systems design, including:

- Customization of service delivery based on a detailed analysis of their needs, worldview, and values.
- Integrating polar opposites such as traditional and alternative healthcare approaches.
- Eliminating bureaucratic systems and replacing them with flow-oriented systems.
- Embracing non-linear systems.[51]

According to Futurist Steve McDonald,

> *We can expect disruptive technologies to radically transform many systems and industries over the next 15 years, including manufacturing and supply systems, energy generation, medicine, transport, and economics among others. It's fair to assume that no aspect of life will remain untouched. New technologies will come with challenges and it's important to align their use with our emerging values, focusing on respecting, supporting, and sustaining humanity and our planet's natural systems.*[52]

New systems will function in paradox and use an "and-and" approach rather than the "either-or" approach so prevalent today.

Instead of one right answer and one right perspective, new systems and solutions will include multiple perspectives, choosing the best from all possibilities in a productive way. This helps create a connection between all groups in society based on common values and norms.

Instead of aiming for consensus and perfection, we'll aim for workable and flexible "good-enough-for-now" solutions. It's going to be more about freedom than how it "has" to be.

And if you think systems like these are something decades off in the future, guess again. There are individuals and organizations who are making change today, and some are operating from the Yellow layer.

So, how do we get there?

Instead of one right answer and one right perspective, new systems and solutions will include multiple perspectives, choosing the best from all possibilities in a productive way.

For Agents for Change, it starts by creating a clear vision and being able to share it with others.

In change theory, there are two common ways to lead change. You can either create a burning platform, which means painting a compelling picture of the crash that will happen if people don't change. Or, you can paint a compelling picture of where you are going and how it will be better than where you are now.

There are plenty of burning-platform scenarios out there right now and they are driven by fear. I prefer to approach change, and life in general, from a place of love and creating the picture of a compelling future. Love is vision, possibility, and hope.

You don't ignore the actual burning platforms, but you focus on building the bridge to the beautiful bountiful garden ahead. You want to move because it's nicer *there*. Not simply because it's horrible *here*.

Michael Bernard Beckwith wisely says, *"Pain pushes you, until your vision pulls you."* Unfortunately, pain is what's pushing many of us now. The pain of fear about the future and what might happen, anxiety about our current situations. This pain can be paralyzing and overwhelming at times.[53] Beckwith also created a process for clarifying your vision that I have used for many years called "The Life Visioning Process."

Instead of pain, we can shift our focus to possibility. Afterall, in a world where there is no one right answer, there are also fewer *wrong* ones. This can be scary, but also very liberating depending on your focus. And the good news is that we get to choose our focus.

The more clarity you can create around your vision, given these parameters, the better. Creating a clear vision when there is much uncertainty requires an acceptance of that uncertainty. You will make mistakes, will need to experiment, and must be open to diverse perspectives. A powerful vision is one that's inspiring and compelling for change, but that is open enough to allow for the unexpected.

Creating this vision won't happen in a vacuum either. Engage others in creating the vision, ensuring you have diverse perspectives. It's easy to involve diverse perspectives when everyone agrees, but your solutions won't be as strong. If you develop a vision from only a Green perspective, it likely won't be appealing for those perceiving the world through a Blue or Orange lens, and you will experience resistance. Polarity Mapping® is a useful tool for considering other perspectives. I cover this in more depth in Chapter 10.

The good news is that we're already seeing plenty of these new systems.

Our successful recycling system in my hometown of Portland, Oregon, demonstrates the transition into Green, while engaging every layer. While far from perfect and although recycling's nothing new, it's been effective at increasing composting and reducing the amount of waste in our landfills.

Here's how it works. The City of Portland owns the garbage collection service. This isn't the case in every city. To encourage people to recycle and compost, the City picks up our recycling and compost bins every week, while only picking up the garbage bins every two weeks. There is also a deposit on bottles and cans in the State of Oregon. As in other states with this deposit system, you pay 10 cents per bottle at the checkout register and get the money back when you return the empties to a designated location.

This combined system engages individuals in every value system layer: Orange and Blue participate, otherwise their garbage cans will overflow. Plus, Blue wants to follow the rules, and Orange wants to get their bottle and can deposits back, so are willing to recycle.

Green usually recycles because they believe it's good for the planet. And, as people have grown accustomed to recycling, the program expands. When people become more aware of how much waste they are generating, and they look for ways to reduce it, be more diligent, and find new ways to use recycled materials.

Once society's dominant layer is Yellow, recycling will likely be an integral part of our life. That's because this layer functions in a "regenerative economy," one that gives appropriate value to our principal capital—the earth and the sun. This system prioritizes sustainable materials, creates very little waste and utilizes recycled and scrap materials when possible. Products are also designed to have a longer lifespan and multiple uses, unlike the plastic and poorly-made dollar-store treasures that are so much a part of today's society. (I can't wait for that!)

—

EXERCISE: Systems Design

Make a list of our current systems that no longer seem to be working. Some examples might be:

- ❖ Healthcare
- ❖ Education
- ❖ Justice
- ❖ Waste disposal
- ❖ Financial
- ❖ Political
- ❖ Social Services
- ❖ Prison
- ❖ Food

Identify one or two systems that you feel most passionate about changing. Now, break it down. Specifically, what aspects of these systems are no longer working? It's also important to note what aspects are working. Remember: as we move into the next layer, it's tempting to throw out everything from the previous layer and replace it. The magic happens when you can identify the things that are working and build from there.

Think about how you could use these concepts, along with your understanding of The Change Code, to design a system.

Designing the Future

Once you have the lay of the land, begin thinking about how a Green system might look? A Yellow System?

What are signs that a new layer is already emerging?

What are some ways we could help ease the transition?

Now, let's tap into possibility.

What could these systems look like? Focus on the one that is most compelling for you. If it seems too large, focus on one aspect of the system.

If you could wave a magic wand today, what would you create?

Think big and for now, don't get distracted by "how" something would happen. Only focus on creating the vision.

For example, how would a Green educational system look? A Yellow educational system? What would a Green justice system look like? A Yellow justice system? A Green healthcare system? A Yellow healthcare system? And so on for any systems in society that stand out for you. Flip back to Chapter 3 if you need to review the different layers.

Here are some examples to help get you started:

Our Healthcare System

What's not working:

Our current healthcare system in the United States focuses on treating the illness, not on staying healthy. Many people don't have health insurance and can't afford to see the doctor when they need to. When individuals get diagnosed with cancer or other serious conditions, many end up in bankruptcy. Pharmaceuticals are very expensive, and some people have to choose between food and taking their medication. Our physicians and caregivers are also experiencing record rates of burnout, depression, and suicide. We've become overspecialized in medicine, which causes the system to lose sight of the whole person.

What is working:
We have advanced technology and are able to cure more diseases than ever before. We have significantly extended the expected lifespan for humans (although it has started to decline again).

Signs of Green:
There's a reconnection with nature as natural medicine grows in popularity. We also see an increase in healthy, plant-based and mindful eating practices.

What would a Green healthcare system look like?
Green is focused on healing the self and the planet, so a Green healthcare system would focus on wellness and preventing disease, instead of only treating it once it occurs. It would be holistic, incorporating mental health, spiritual health, relationships, and our environment, along with our physical health.

A Green system would offer the best of natural medicine, Eastern medicine, nutrition, massage, and energy work, along with traditional Western medicine. Instead of having a primary care physician, we would have a care team who collaborate to treat the whole person. Members of the team would include a wellness coach and a nutritionist to support us with our eating habits to maximize the benefits. It may also include a spiritual mentor or mindset coach.

Green is very inclusive so there would be healthcare for all. It would ensure that care is appropriate for the individual so we would see culturally and gender-identity appropriate care, as well as trauma-informed care.

Signs of Yellow:

We are beginning to see new types of providers that offer the best of Eastern and Western medicine, including nutrition and mindfulness. We are also seeing highly-personalized medicine such as individual medication dosing based on your DNA and personal attributes.

Other examples of major system changes can be seen in our judicial and educational systems.

A Green Judicial System:

In Alaska, a new type of Judicial System is emerging for drug and alcohol addiction. It's called Wellness Court, and it's a therapeutic court run as a collaboration between the state and the local native tribes. It's actually helping addicted people who've committed crimes recover without going to prison.

Participants may be referred to the therapeutic court after conviction but before sentencing. Those who successfully complete the 18-month program may see a reduction in their sentence. For those who fail, original sentencing is immediate. The program has been highly successful and is modeled after a similar program in Minnesota.[54]

A Green Educational System:

In Finland, education is free (including school lunches) and is a constitutional right. This inclusiveness is a Green trait.

Children spend their early years playing and don't start school until they are seven. There is only one standardized test for students, and it's taken at the end of high school. Students have far less homework than they do in America, and there is a low rate of dropout.

In high school, students have the choice of taking one of two paths: a general education path that prepares them for college, or a vocational route with apprenticeships that prepare them for employment. They can also change paths if they choose.

Finnish teachers are highly valued and allowed to develop their own grading systems. They are required to have a master's degree unless they are vocational teachers. College is free and adult education is promoted and subsidized. The value placed on humans is key to a Green system.[55]

Since 1993, another Scandinavian country, Denmark, gives students empathy training one hour per week in a practice called *"Klassens tid"*. They learn to help their classmates and to only compete with themselves. This subject is treated with the same importance as science or math.

> *During the Klassens tid students discuss their problems, either related to school or not, and the whole class, together with the teacher, tries to find a solution based on real listening and understanding. If there are no problems to discuss, children simply spend the time together relaxing and enjoying hygge, a word (and also a verb and an adjective), which cannot be translated literally, since it is a phenomenon* **closely related to Danish culture**. *Hygge could be defined as "intentionally created intimacy".*[56]

Perhaps Denmark's regular ranking as one of the happiest countries in the world has roots in this training.[57]

Now that you have your list of areas for change and have created a big vision for at least one system, are there ways you can share your vision with others?

Are there ways you can help make that vision a reality?

Write down at least one action step you can take.

In summary

To create change, we first need to let go of what is crumbling—gracefully. The complex problems of our world require new ways of problem-solving. Leading this change requires patience, new skills, and an understanding of whole systems thinking. It also requires having a clear vision you can share with others. Look at what's not working and then imagine what could work... what could be possible.

OK, now you've thought about the types of things that will need to change, in the next chapters, I'll provide you with the tools and information to make those changes a reality.

CHAPTER 6

Inner Work for Change

We do not need magic to change the world, we carry all the power we need inside ourselves already: we have the power to imagine better.

~J.K. ROWLING

Imagine driving home in gridlock traffic after a long, hectic day. You're tired and hungry, your patience is running low, and you're a half-hour late for your daughter's ballet recital. A guy in a silver sports car pulls up next to you and swerves into your lane. You slam on your breaks to prevent rear-ending him and your drink goes flying. You swear and honk your horn at the jerk. *Jeez! He should slow down and be more careful! And that was a $4 cappuccino!*

Because you've studied The Change Code, you realize that was just your Red layer poking through. You're usually calm and pleasant in your dominant layer of Green, but, just like the rest of us, your previous layers are still within you, like that Russian doll. And they step out when needed (or think they're needed).

As an Agent for Change, you're self-aware. Thankfully, incidents like this are few and far between, and for the most part, short-lived. You've learned breathing and meditation techniques that keep you grounded most of the time, and you're always working on your own development. Or *are* you?

The First Step: Inner Work

This might come as a relief to some of you and be very agitating to others. But the first thing a leader with a big vision needs to do is get quiet and go within.

Yes, in this chapter we'll go inside and look at your values, the power of meditation and mindset, and your spiritual life. Doing this inner work helps you develop the presence and awareness that is going to allow you to address complex challenges and play the long game of creating change. Believe me, this is crucial, especially when you're working with people and polarizing issues that poke and prod at your own deeply held beliefs.

Gandhi said, *"You must be the change you want to see in the world."* Visionary leaders look outward and see future possibilities, but often overlook the deep work that is necessary for true transformation. So often, these leaders are exhausted, overworked, and carrying the weight of the world on their shoulders.

The Change Code provides a wonderful tool to help you gain new insights about yourself and what's important, as well as your potential blind spots.

Look back to the results of your Change Code assessment for a moment. Remember, that while you have one or two dominant layers, we all contain every layer within us. So, depending on the situation and our immediate environment, you may perceive the world through a Green value system and express other layers, like that Red eruption when you were cut off in traffic. When you clearly recognize the positive and negative expressions of each layer in yourself, you can then see them in others and in society as a whole. I promise, this will save you a lot of time and stress down the road.

As you think back through your life can you notice when you began *expressing* a certain value system and when you actually began *living it* fully?

My Color Story

I grew up in a rural community in Montana. In high school, I became interested in preserving the forests around us even though my family heated our small home with wood. I also began to experience empathy and to feel strong emotions for people and animals struggling around the world. I knew I wanted to make a difference. I started my high school's first competitive debate team, because I believed that it was important to be able to understand and debate both sides of an argument.

While these were signs of Green emerging, I also lived firmly in Orange—believing equally passionately in new jeans, big hair, and fast cars. After graduating from college, I went full-on Orange, which meant I was focused primarily on building my career and increasing my income. I had a young daughter to support and bills to pay.

It wasn't until I was in my thirties that I began to realize the corporate job wasn't working for me anymore. I wanted more balance and found a New Thought church. My value system was definitely shifting. By my late thirties, my life was totally different, and my worldview was much more from the Green layer, while also emerging into Yellow. While I still do corporate work, my primary focus is on finding ways to help heal our planet, support mission-driven leaders, and continuing to heal and develop myself.

To think more about the different colors you hold, check on yourself when you're particularly happy, stressed, or tired. Now that you've learned about The Change Code, you'll probably notice when your various colors come through. Imagine finding out someone has lied to you? Or you're accused of something you haven't done? That wave of revenge, anger, or violence you feel is the spike of Red energy. Or when you're at a football game wearing your team's jersey and cheering them on with thousands of other screaming fans, getting a glimpse of Purple tribal energy.

EXERCISE:

1. Analyze your own beliefs: In the next 24-hours, notice when you have a strong response to something you hear, see, or read. How do you feel? Do you feel like someone did something wrong and you feel judgement? Try to connect your feeling to your own values or beliefs.

2. The next time you hear something you disagree with, assume that the person is a good and intelligent person. Try to the understand the moral foundations that are behind their statements.

Align with Your Values

One of my most important values is a respect for all of nature—and I try to practice this by respecting all living creatures. While I grew up eating meat (not many vegetarians in rural Montana in the late 80s), this began to trouble me several years ago and I reduced my meat consumption. Today, I rarely eat it, although I believe it is possible to eat meat in a way that's still respectful. Moving away from meat has boosted my confidence because I feel more aligned with my own personal values.

One sign of maturity, and definitely of a good leader, is to know your values and to live in alignment with them. Good leaders walk their talk and work toward alignment with their values in every aspect of their lives. They also recognize when they are out of alignment and make the necessary adjustments. You know when you're out of alignment—you feel stress, discomfort, and anxiety, and maybe even become physically ill. Sometimes the cause may be a job, a toxic relationship, bad habits, or where you live.

My friend Meg was dealing with a similar issue recently. She and her husband Joe live very intentionally and try to minimize their carbon footprint. When her husband wanted a big Toyota pick-up, Meg *really* struggled with the idea of owning such a big truck that uses so much fuel. To her, that felt misaligned and lacking integrity. As much as Joe wanted the truck, Meg felt ill every time she imagined it in the driveway. But, since it was so important to her husband, Meg found a way to compromise with Joe. He would get the truck but they would also use it to support a local charity by hauling things, and helping friends and family move as much as they could. She made him promise they'd look for ways to use the truck "for good."

While her values still don't align with the fuel consumption, Meg found a positive purpose and made the best of the decision. The couple enjoys helping people more often, she feels much more aligned with her values, and she can even drive the truck around town without cringing or feeling like she has to explain herself.

When Nelson Mandela was released from prison, he had to do some work on aligning with his values. He's quoted as saying, **"As I walked out the door toward the gate that would lead to my freedom, I knew if I didn't leave my bitterness and hatred behind, I'd still be in prison."** Mandela realized that he needed to forgive in order to live his values and be a true Agent for Change.

It's so important to pause and see where in your life you're aligned and not aligned with your values. Here are some ways to do that:

EXERCISE

Think about all the parts of your life: home, work, family, community, health, spirituality, and finances. What are the areas that feel like they aren't aligned? Take the time to investigate. What are your true values in that area and how can you live more authentically as who you really are?

Read through this list of values and circle the ones that apply to you. Then whittle down your list to your top 5.

Abundance	Enjoyment	Love
Achievement	Faith	Mastery
Adventure	Fame	Mindfulness
Beauty	Family	Peace
Belonging	Fearlessness	Optimism
Bliss	Fun	Open-mindedness
Boldness	Flow	Passion
Celebrity	Freedom	Play
Charity	Grace	Purpose
Charm	Happiness	Realism
Commitment	Harmony	Relationship
Compassion	Health	Relaxation
Connection	Honesty	Sacrifice
Contribution	Humor	Security
Creativity	Independence	Spirituality
Decisiveness	Integrity	Teamwork
Delight	Intelligence	Trust
Dignity	Leadership	Understanding
Duty	Learning	Unity
Education	Joy	Warmth
Energy	Justice	Wisdom

List your values in the table below in the order of importance.

VALUES	BEHAVIOR (Which of your behaviors support this value?)	ALIGNMENT (How aligned are you with this value? How often do your behaviors reflect it in your daily life?)
Play	Scheduling time to play soccer on the weekends and painting ceramics.	I make some time to play but I'd like to do more. I only play a few times per month but I'd like to either play soccer or paint every week.

Practice:
What can you do to live in closer alignment with your values?

If there are areas in your life where you are not currently aligned with your values, what changes can you make?

How do your values line up with your Change Code layer? Flip back to Chapter 3 or your assessment results from www.TheChangeCode.net if you need a refresher.

OK, let's keep going with the inner work. Paying attention to your mindset and learning to listen to your inner wisdom is incredibly important for Agents for Change. When you are open-minded, you have the capacity to function at more complex levels and are better able to solve problems. This is the healthiest mindset and gives you the best opportunity to see possibilities in the world. A closed mindset limits the number of possibilities you can see. It may be the result of trauma and causes you to feel fear and want to stay put.

Good leaders understand the importance of growth and learning, and aren't afraid to make mistakes. Through your own actions and habits, you can literally rewire your brain, which allows you to grow and change. Dr. Carol Dweck coined the terms **fixed mindset** and **growth mindset** following her research about why some students were devastated by even small setbacks, while others were not. Some students think their intelligence level is fixed and difficult to change. But she found that when students believe they can grow—that they can get smarter and that their efforts make them stronger—they put in more time and effort, resulting in higher achievement and less concern about setbacks.

This difference in mindset turns out to have a profound impact on your behavior, and even on your ability to learn and succeed. Research in neuroscience shows that we can increase the neural growth in our brain with good nutrition, using good strategies, asking questions, and practicing.

Dweck found that when students were taught about growth mindset, their academic results improved over time. Students with a growth mindset seek to "learn at all times". They constantly stretch themselves and take on new challenges. Whereas students with a fixed mindset focus on "looking smart at all times." They avoid looking deficient in the eyes of others so stay within their comfort zones.

With a growth mindset, you're open to possibilities, new perspectives, and to acknowledge and learn when we're wrong or make mistakes. Increase your growth mindset by stepping out of your comfort zone, trying new things, and viewing mistakes as learning opportunities.[58] Nelson Mandela created a great mantra that you can practice:

I never lose. I either win or learn.

Graves also wrote about this concept by describing open, arrested, and closed personalities. A closed personality is indicated by someone who isn't able to change, and consequently displays inappropriate behavior, overreacts to frustration, and may be inflexible and insatiable. An arrested personality has the potential for growth but is temporarily caught in life conditions that create barriers to change. An open personality according to Graves:

...tends to change as the world changes and changes the world as his open personality changes.[59]

Cultivate Creativity and Intuition

Intuition and creativity will become even more critical as humans emerge from the very left-brain-centric culture of Orange. We're not going to solve problems with black and white solutions or by analyzing data and facts alone. It will require innovation, creativity, and intuition.

Cultivating these skills will improve your ability to lead, as well as to solve problems. Hone your intuition by staying present and learning to recognize when it's trying to get your attention—whether it's a dream, synchronicity, a feeling in your gut, or a deep sense of knowing. Once you recognize an intuitive hit, learning to trust it and act on it is the next thing.

A key aspect of the transition from Green to Yellow is learning how to distinguish feelings of fear from intuitive insights, which are also often experienced as a feeling.

Keep an open mind and avoid labeling things as right or wrong. Did you know that once you judge something as "bad," you remove it from the potential ingredients for a creative solution? One of the strengths of Yellow is that it doesn't limit itself to one system or philosophy. Instead, it remains open to all possibilities, taking the best aspects from many different perspectives to develop unique solutions.

You can also access your intuition through a regular meditation practice, and by asking questions to God or the Universe (whatever term feels right to you) and listening for the answer. You can also pose a question and then allow yourself to write the response using stream of consciousness writing—not over-thinking it, just allowing it to flow.

Meditate

The best leaders are mindful and present, and know their strengths as well as their limitations. They stay centered in the face of conflict, don't take things too personally, and trust their intuition. If you want to be a more conscious leader, a regular meditation practice helps maintain this state, and also increases feelings of empathy and compassion—necessary traits for your transition to the next layer.

Spirituality

I was tempted to leave spirituality out of this book. I feared it would be polarizing. But then I looked at how significant it's been in my own development as a leader (I first heard about Spiral Dynamics at *church*, for goodness sake!), and as I interviewed other leaders that I admire, I found that it was equally important to them as well. Spirituality is one of my values, so to mention it helps me stay aligned.

Spirituality doesn't have to be part of a formalized religion, but it is a connection to something greater, a source, God, Yahweh, Allah, the Universe, or whatever term you choose to use. Developing this aspect of ourselves gives life meaning, optimism, and helps us feel a greater connection to others.

Part of my own growth has been to recognize the common threads of world religions and to see that spirituality and faith are not the same as religion. Religion has historically fueled polarization, particularly through war, but it doesn't have to. Religions, like all aspects of humanity, have the capacity to adapt to changing conditions.

Pope Francis, for instance, has been very vocal about the need to address climate change, taking a Green stance while still representing a traditionally Blue religious structure that is demonstrating signs of growth. He said, "We are not faced with two separate crises, one environmental and the other social, but rather one complex crisis which is both social and environmental...the exploitation of the planet has already exceeded acceptable limits and we still have not solved the problem of poverty."[60]

Practice Extreme Self-Care

"I spend my life building the world I want to live in"
~ROBIN CHASE

Hopefully, you're doing your inner work and feeling more aligned, clear, and tuned in to your intuition. But to lead transformational change, you must be grounded. And that's not going to happen when you're exhausted, eating poorly, or constantly stressed, like so many leaders today. It's like the announcement they make when you fly on a plane—put on your own oxygen mask before you help others. You can't fill the cups of others when your own cup is empty. And you can only push yourself so much before you collapse. This is why self-care is so extremely important now.

Self-care is way more than massage or a candlelit bath—it includes eating right, exercising, getting enough sleep, and maintaining positive and fulfilling relationships with your friends and family. And it's also about scheduling those things that help you manage your own energy like setting healthy boundaries, spending time in nature, doing yoga, and developing that regular mindfulness and meditation practice.

When you create a regular self-care routine, you have a better chance at making it a consistent practice. These routines will look different for everyone and may change over time. You'll need to experiment to find what works best for you, but do it. Schedule it and make it a top priority.

Gabby Bernstein, an author and spiritual leader who displays some Second-Tier traits, recently shared her morning routine on Instagram. She said the routine is what allows her to do the work that she does and that she can't ease up on it, even when she's traveling or speaking at events. It's a non-negotiable. When she's busy, she knows that she'll need to get up earlier.

Gabby says, "For me and the career path that I've chosen, my health, wellbeing, and energy are the most important thing to me. In order for me to be of service in the way I want to be, I have to be healthy, I have to be happy, I have to be free of anxiety and fear. And so, I have to make my morning and night routines very, very sacred."

Her morning routine includes a warm drink of water, lemon, apple cider vinegar and a drop of coconut oil first thing in the morning to wake up her digestive system. She also has a 20-minute tapping meditation (Emotional Freedom Technique), mantras and affirmations, and a yoga and exercise routine.[61]

Some good resources for self-care include, *Extreme Self Care* by Cheryl Richardson, and the Buddify or Headspace apps for Meditation.

If you think you're too busy to take care of yourself, remember something else Gandhi said:

I have so much to accomplish today that I must meditate for two hours instead of one.

In summary

Good leaders understand the importance of learning and having a growth mindset. They practice self-care. They know and align with their values, and attempt to understand the values of those they communicate with. They embrace their spirituality and make time for daily rituals and routines that foster their creativity and intuition.

You've seen why it's important to start on the inside when there's big work to do. Now let's look at how to become an Agent for Change.

CHAPTER 7

How to Become an
Agent for Change

What you do makes a difference, and you have to decide
what kind of difference you want to make.
~JANE GOODALL

You might have a picture of a traditional "leader" in your mind. Someone who's gained their position by using a combination of strength, charisma, strong opinions, and polished public speaking skills. Someone able to mobilize their like-minded tribe. Or someone who's advanced by merit, being seen as the most capable—or at least the most capable option available. These have been the qualities we value in our leaders.

Here's the problem with traditional leadership, though: Our problems have become so complex that an individual cannot possibly have all the solutions. Today's new leaders, who I call Agents for Change, gather groups of experts who work together to find solutions.

> These leaders can see a bigger vision for humanity and the world, but know they can't get there alone.

Leaders who limit themselves to inspiring only the *like-minded* will soon find themselves struggling. Agents for Change engage and inspire people who have diverse backgrounds and values.

Agents for Change are comfortable in their own skin, because they know their strengths and values, as well as their limitations and blind spots. They easily bring together a wide range of people and groups who come up with unique solutions that support *everyone*. These leaders can see a bigger vision for humanity and the world, but know they can't get there alone. They understand that they will need to collaborate with other people and organizations to accomplish anything meaningful. They don't lead from a place of ego or control but with a sense of purpose and a desire to bring out the best in individuals, humanity, and the planet.

So who are Agents for Change? An Agent for Change is anyone committed to making the world a better place, helping lead positive change, and doing the inner work to be a light on our path.

They are visionary leaders, healers, artists, activists, inventors, educators, ministers, writers, and other creators who are pulled to service and a higher calling. Whether they work at an organization, lead a non-profit, or volunteer in their community, they believe in the inherent good in humanity and help bring that good out in others.

As I talk about change leadership in this book, it's important to recognize that we can all be leaders, *wherever* we are. We can lead within our homes, our workplaces, our places of worship, and our neighborhoods. We don't have to be voted in, hired, or "appointed" by anyone. Becoming a leader in this movement only requires one thing: That you make the choice and commit to being an Agent for Change.

In this complex world, problems and solutions are not simple or black and white. So, rather than using traditional *either-or* frameworks, Agents for Change embrace the *and*, considering both *what* needs to be done and *how* it can best be implemented. They can handle uncertainty and meld the best aspects of multiple ideas and theories to form something completely new. They actively engage others in a way that fully leverages their talents and contributions. They understand the different value layers and focus on win/win solutions for all. Mindful and authentic people naturally trust them.

Beck and Cowan call these new, emerging leaders "spiral wizards" because they understand The Change Code. They are able to navigate all the colors, putting the right people or teams in the right places, at the right time.

The time has come for us to train, promote, and BE this kind of leader. And we need to support and vote for these leaders when they step forward.

Going back to the 7 Principles, you've already committed to leading and understanding the Change Code values system. You know how important inner work and extreme self-care are for your energy and grounding as you navigate our polarized world. In this chapter, we'll look at the rest of the principles and how to practice them in daily life.

Understand the Group You are Trying to Help

If you've ever tried to help someone, you know that many times your efforts to help others fall flat. One big reason for this is that you don't really understand who you are trying to help. For instance, what are their value systems and specific challenges? The good news is that by using the Change Code you're better able to meet people where they are, and are more likely to deliver the type of assistance they need.

For example, if you work for a non-profit that helps the homeless, you'll be far more successful when you understand that homeless individuals often naturally regress to the Beige layer. When you're homeless, finding food, staying safe, and meeting basic needs are paramount. And the Beige value system has a very different sense of time—focused on the moment and immediate needs, not on long-term planning.

However, many programs designed to help the homeless have limited hours of operation and may be in hard-to-reach locations for someone without a car. That makes it challenging for people who could use the help to take advantage of the resources that are available. Also, there are programs that focus on resume-building or job interview skills—long-term solutions that are not so meaningful when you don't know where you're going to sleep tonight.

A program called Built for Zero is hoping to change all that, and they're doing it through the use of data. One of their stated goals is "Helping communities adopt proven best practices, deploy existing resources more efficiently, and use real-time data to improve performance."

Built for Zero uses sophisticated analytics software to track the needs and locations of homeless people, facilitating individualized solutions as agencies help them into housing. Until now, agencies only had generic census data to measure the rate of homelessness in a community. Built for Zero uses seven key data points to create a near real-time dashboard for the homeless people in an area, and shares it with local leaders tasked with solving the problem. They also engage the government and private sectors to secure resources, and connect communities to facilitate group problem solving.

This initiative is a great example of understanding the people you are trying to help and meeting them where they are.

So far, the program says three municipalities have ended what it terms "chronic homelessness" where people have been living rough for more than a year: Bergen County, New Jersey; Lancaster, Pennsylvania; and Rockford, Illinois. Nine cities – the latest being Abilene, Texas – have ended homelessness among military veterans, one of the hardest-to-reach groups, using Built for Zero.[62]

The Need for a Better Understanding in the Middle East

Dr. Don Beck and Elza Maalouf, author of *Emerge!: The Rise of Functional Democracy and the Future of the Middle East*, led major initiatives to improve relations in and between countries in that region, which has Red and Blue dominant value systems. Beck and Maalouf engaged with a group of Palestinian women, and asked them why efforts by the United Nations and NGOs (which operate primarily from the Orange and Green value systems) haven't helped their situation.

What they found is that the programs funded to help the Palestinian women had unrealistic expectations and conditions that didn't fit the culture or value systems of the community. A better understanding of the existing value systems, cultures, and norms may have produced better results.

Butheina, leader of a local Palestinian organization said:

We are tired of them pushing their women empowerment training on us without providing opportunities to create sustainable jobs and solid careers. The abstract concepts are fine, but they are not helping us create businesses, or helping our children learn computer skills. They force us to spend hundreds of thousands of dollars on restaurants, hotels and seminars and refuse to give us part of the money to build a small center to train women and children on how to use the computer.

There are two young girls who hold degrees in education and computer science who have been looking for a job for the last 7 months to no avail. They just want to work and make a living… Not learn about Democracy and Governance in seminars while not having a job or a place to exercise "Governance".[63]

The well-meaning programs embodied Green value structures and requirements for participation rather than helping the women in this contentious environment find ways to thrive in a Red/Blue-dominant society. Even though the program leaders had the best of intentions, learning success skills geared toward their actual environment would have helped these women much more.

Remember the Change Code rule: individuals and societies must pass through each layer in the same order. If a community is in a different layer than yours, the point isn't to "fix" that. Instead, it's to help people thrive within that value system while the community evolves. As I'm sure you've seen in your own life, imposing values from one layer onto another just doesn't work.

While you may not be leading major initiatives in the Middle East, the concept applies to other, less complicated, situations as well.

Have you ever tried to suggest that someone who loves using plastic bags for his groceries start using a cloth bag instead? Or suggest that someone who reveres her physician and Western medicine try acupuncture? Your suggestion may not be received well. Understanding someone's worldview, as well as the limitations of your own, can help you communicate better with others.

What to Do About Extremism

Many leaders are stumped when they face extremism in their own communities. The growth of extremism has increased polarization in society, is inflammatory, and prevents the open communication and dialogue that is absolutely necessary for finding workable solutions.

Extremists hurt everyone in society and create even more polarization and disruption. Even if their intentions are good, those with extreme views on the right or left leave out anyone with different views. While extremists may succeed for a short time, when a large percentage of the population feels left out of the system, there is always a backlash and a movement back the other way.

Agents for Change understand the need to denounce extremism. After Mandela's release from prison, but before his election in 1994, Chris Hani, a popular black leader fighting for equal rights, was shot and killed by a white right-wing extremist. The assassination understandably evoked an outburst of anger from the black community. They wanted revenge. Instead of revenge, however, Mandela asked the community to unify in the face of adversity. Here is part of his statement:

Tonight, I am reaching out to every single South African, black and white, from the very depths of my being. A white man, full of prejudice and hate, came to our country and committed a deed so foul that our whole nation now teeters on the brink of disaster... The cold-blooded murder of Chris Hani has sent shock waves throughout the country and the world... Now is the time for all South Africans to stand together against those who, from any quarter, wish to destroy what Chris Hani gave his life for—the freedom of all of us.[64]

Mandela recognized the shooter as an extremist, denounced his behavior, and reminded everyone that they share the collective goal of freedom. Instead of creating further division, Mandela instead reminded people to unite in the cause of their common aspiration.

Can you think of other leaders who demonstrate unity instead of divisiveness?

Engage Others in Something Bigger than All of Us

The term Superordinate Goals was coined by Turkish-American social psychologist Muzafer Sherif and his famous Robbers Cave Experiment, in which two groups of boys in a camp were pitted against each other in various games, creating animosity between the groups. Tension between the boys eased when the two groups cooperated and moved toward a shared goal.

Superordinate Goals are goals that are created and shared by individuals from different groups. Some refer to them as "overarching" or "shared" goals. They require collaboration and cooperation. It might be something we are trying to achieve, or a shared enemy that we must work together to defeat or defend against.

The world of sports often creates Superordinate Goals. Diverse individuals come together to watch sporting events and cheer on their local team. People from all walks of life, who might have very different social or political views, wear the same team shirts and hats, and yell the same cheers as they hope for victory.

Mandela united all South Africans around the country's Springbok rugby team as a Superordinate Goal.[65] During Apartheid, the national rugby team, the Springboks, only appealed to whites. They were also considered underdogs in the league.

However, Mandela supported the team and set out to spread the love for rugby to all South Africans. 1994 marked the end of Apartheid and in 1995, South Africa hosted the Rugby World Cup. They weren't expected to perform well but South Africa was the host country that year and the team's drive and determination took them to victory.

Black and white communities shared the slogan, "One team, One country." All of a sudden, they had a shared hero. Against all odds, the Springboks ended up winning the World Cup that year, resulting in a major celebration across the nation. Their victory was a victory for all South Africans and everyone celebrated, together, in the streets. More than just a sporting event, the World Cup served to unite a nation.

You can learn more about these efforts in the movie *Invictus*, or by reading Dr. Don Beck's book, *The Crucible*, which tells the story of his work with Mandela and his 67 trips to South Africa.[66]

Superordinate Goals can also involve a shared enemy. This was definitely the case during the Cold War, a period from 1946-1989 involving high levels of tension between the United States (Orange capitalism) and the Soviet Union (Blue communism).[67]

And no one will forget the aftermath of the terrorist attacks on September 11, 2001 when almost 3,000 people were killed on U.S. soil. This horrible event brought the American people together in ways that hadn't happened in over a generation, unifying us against a shared enemy.

If you look at the polarization we're experiencing today, you'll see that there isn't a Superordinate Goal to unite folks on both sides of almost any topic, particularly the current political parties. There are certainly issues that *should* bring us together, like climate change and immigration. These and other Wicked Problems are only going to be solved by large-scale collaboration, led by Agents for Change.

AntFarm:
Creating Community Through
Superordinate Goals

L ocated between a gun store and a chainsaw shop on a busy thoroughfare in the small town of Sandy, Oregon, AntFarm is a growing non-profit making a positive impact in the region. AntFarm is the result of one man, Nunpa (a Lakota nickname for his formal name, Two Foxes Singing), bringing together individuals with diverse values and backgrounds in the community to solve a shared problem—troubled youth and a lack of opportunities for young people.

Nunpa used to commute through Sandy from his home on Mount Hood to his job as an occupational therapist working with at-risk youth in downtown Portland. Nearly every morning, he would see young people on the streets of Sandy at 5 or 6:00 am. They had been out all night and didn't appear to be on their way to work or school. The outlook for their future was less than positive.

Nunpa asked himself, "Wouldn't it be great to create opportunities for these young people?" He knew of an empty building in disrepair on Sandy's main street. Nunpa saw the potential for the building and for the community and decided to take a risk, leaving his full-time job.

He hired a group of young people, got some buy-in from the building owner, and they began remodeling. He started a non-profit and began engaging the community, one by one and conversation by conversation. By the end of the summer, AntFarm was open for business. It started off as a small café, bakery, and coffee shop that would bring in money to help the city's youth, while also providing jobs.

Led by a small but diverse board of community members with very different religious and political views, the group agreed on the need to support youth in the community. This became the launchpad for a wide range of services including:

- A free/donation-based home-repair program for the elderly in the community, creating connections between two vulnerable populations, the youth and the elderly

- No-cost summer programs for youth, including camping and hiking trips, writing and art classes, and job-training

- Tutoring services in the back of the café

- State and federal contracts for creating and maintaining trails in the mountains around Sandy

- A community farmer's market

- A community recycling program that also raises

money for AntFarm

Today, a sign hangs in the café that says:

> AntFarm is a non-profit founded in 1998. Our
> vision is to create and build a stronger, more con-
> nected community, in which EVERY person lives
> with health, purpose, and hope. AntFarm opened
> its doors in 2013. Since then, over 1,000 youth
> have come through, 300+ employed, and 600+
> seniors have been served.

When I spoke to Nunpa on a recent visit, he said:

> We're redefining community. AntFarm welcomes
> everyone without judgement and we work
> together to help and serve. In return, those who
> participate learn new job skills and a work ethic,
> receive help with their homework, and become
> part of a supportive community, perhaps for
> the first time in their lives. When you come into
> the café on Tuesdays, you'll see a group of elders
> having a Bible study next to a table of youth in an
> LGBT meeting.

AntFarm demonstrates the power of Superordinate
Goals—engaging diverse groups to come together
toward a common goal.

In summary

As an Agent for Change, you'll go a lot further when you understand the group you're trying to help by learning The Change Code, denouncing extremism, finding ways to create unity instead of divisiveness, and identifying Superordinate Goals that everyone can believe in.

I'm not saying any of this is easy, but I do have some fantastic tools for you. In the next chapter, I'll show you how to find common ground even in challenging situations—and be an Agent for Change even on social media.

CHAPTER 8

Finding Common Ground and Reclaiming Social Media

If you don't know the guy on the other side of the world, love him anyway because he's just like you. He has the same dreams, the same hopes and fears. It's one world, pal. We're all neighbors.

~FRANK SINATRA

The idea of helping people find common ground in modern-day America was a major impetus for writing this book. After all, how are we supposed to solve some of the world's biggest challenges when we can't talk with each other or agree on what should be done? Sometimes, we can't even define what the problem is.

When I ask people in workshops I lead and in my Facebook group, Agents for Change (www.facebook.com/groups/thechangecode) what they most want to learn, "how to find common ground" is the most common answer.

As I was writing this book, I heard many stories from people who've been directly affected by polarization in their own lives and families. There's my friend Christine whose husband had too many heated political arguments during family holiday dinners. These arguments have made the relationships so uncomfortable that Christine and her husband rarely speak to his family now and never attend family holiday celebrations together.

And if you're on Facebook, you've undoubtedly seen or been part of a less-than-friendly interaction over politics or some news story. People have blocked or unfriended friends they've known for years because of their comments or posts.

So how do we begin to ease this tension, and bring people back together?

The first step is to look at what's going on beneath the surface, at what's driving people's emotions. When people disagree about something, they often have differing fears and beliefs resulting from their underlying value systems. At first glance, it may seem like these differences are too far apart for any common ground to be had.

As humans, we crave certainty and consistency. We want to know which answer is the right answer, and which answer is the wrong answer. So, when there are two opposing views, we tend to naturally pick one side or the other, rather than looking for the common ground and unique solutions in between. Agents for Change are able to handle uncertainty and work to build bridges between people, between races, and between political viewpoints.

Let's look at the issue of gun ownership in America, a Wicked Problem if ever there was one. This issue often gets divided into two camps, Second Amendment supporters who believe in the right to bear arms, and the Gun Control supporters, who believe that gun-ownership should be more regulated for the common good. The reality is that this is a complex issue and most people aren't fully aligned with one side or the other, but are somewhere in the middle. You'll often find people are less divided when the questions are specific: Does the Constitution guarantee the right to own assault rifles and bump stocks? Should there be stronger background checks when purchasing firearms?

In recent polls, more than 90% of Americans support universal background checks for firearms. So why aren't we able to pass legislation?[68]

Getting to the root cause is critical for identifying the common ground. Because without knowing the root cause of why someone believes what they do, you might debate all day and feel like you're going in circles. Have you ever felt like that when you're talking with someone on the other side of an issue like gun control?

Understanding the differences in layers which we discussed in Chapter 3 can be helpful in identifying the root cause for the disagreement and make it much easier to talk with someone on the "other side of the aisle."

This was something Nelson Mandela understood when he was President of South Africa. He also understood the importance of value systems from the work of Clare W. Graves. Mandela wanted to end apartheid without a civil war.

While it would have been easy to assume that apartheid was caused entirely by racism, Mandela knew that racism could be thought of as a symptom of a deeper reality. The root causes of apartheid were the different value systems among the various groups and tribes in the country.

Mandela helped unite the tribes by identifying the common ground they shared—they were all South Africans. He brought this national pride out through the use of sport and his support of the Springbok rugby team. Mandela also framed his message based on the different value systems.

Guidelines for Finding Common Ground

Finding common ground, even with people who diametrically oppose you, begins with having a meaningful dialogue. Research has shown that the most powerful thing to help people overcome their biases, refine their opinions, and build community is *genuine* conversation with people *they respect.*

Having conversations with people from different perspectives helps you see things you can't see on your own. We all have blind spots in our thinking, and it's human nature to think we're right. Diverse perspectives help us make better decisions.

Agents for Change know this and surround themselves with smart people with a wide range of perspectives. Abraham Lincoln even appointed his greatest political opponents to his cabinet, creating his "team of rivals." He knew, even if he didn't agree with them, their perspectives would be helpful for making wise decisions.

Let's go over some things to keep in mind when having a meaningful dialog with someone. **Some basic guidelines for finding common ground are:**

1. **Relax and center yourself.** Make sure you are calm and grounded before the conversation. If you are feeling scattered or upset, those emotions will show and make it more difficult for a calm discussion.

2. **Create an environment for conversation.** A calm and trusting environment is best for this type of discussion. Put away your cell phone and remove other distractions.

3. **Always be respectful and avoid criticism.** In Dale Carnegie's famous book, *How to Win Friends and Influence People*, he says,

   Criticism is futile because it puts a person on the defensive and usually makes him strive to justify himself.

4. **Establish shared ground rules:** This helps create a sense of safety and trust. Some examples of ground rules might include: staying present in the moment, not interrupting each other, share the time, only speak for yourself and don't try to represent a group or political party, be curious about where the conversation could go, don't be too critical, and respect each other's differences.

5. **Be prepared to have a dialogue**. Speak and listen to another person with an open heart and an open mind that isn't blocked by the veil of your own world view. Remember it's a two-way conversation and that you're not trying to change the other person's viewpoint. It's about finding areas of agreement that can serve as the starting point for a discussion. Remember, with Wicked Problems, there is no one right, easy solution. It's about navigating the issue to find workable solutions for right now and continuing to work through issues as they arise.

6. **Listen and understand the other person's perspective**—why do they believe what they believe? The "why" is really important. If you don't know, just ask. Understand their value system.

7. **When possible, provide validation** for the other person. Validation means finding and affirming a "kernel of truth" in another person's perspective or situation. It's acknowledging that the emotions and thoughts are true for that person, even if you don't think or feel the same way. If you're on the other side of the issue from the gun-owner I just mentioned, for example, you might say something like, "I relate to you wanting to keep your family safe."

8. **Know and share values and fears,** and when possible, think and talk at the level of *values*. What do you believe and why? Don't just share political party rhetoric and salacious headlines that were designed to get clicks. One way to do this is to each share personal stories about your commitment to the issue and the change you want to see in the world. This process helps create understanding, empathy, trust, and connections on a human level.

9. **Identify shared ideals.** When you begin to have discussions, you will undoubtedly find areas where you agree. Identify and

build upon those. For example, we all want a healthy and safe world for our children to grow up in. Start there.

10. **Create opportunities for shared learning.** Learning new things together can create possibilities that go beyond past disagreements. Some areas for shared learning may include studying the history of a specific issue, reading a book about specific theories or beliefs, taking a class, or attending a lecture.

11. **Agree on a shared source for validating facts** when there's a question on either side. Some good ones include:

    • **PolitiFact:** a non-partisan fact-checking website that focuses on claims made in the political sphere in the US. This includes statements by politicians, political topics such as immigration, and general news.

    • **Factcheck.org:** a fact-checking website with an established history of journalistic rigor, but it is also one of the partners Facebook has recruited to combat viral fake news.

Many of us may do these things naturally in our business or working with others. If you want more ideas for how to find common ground, check out the YOUTUBE channel called Jubilee. This group brings together individuals with diverse perspectives to discuss polarizing issues such as abortion, gun control, immigration, veganism, religion, and more.

They start the discussion with the two groups standing on opposite sides of the room, with a number of chairs in the middle. Then they begin to ask questions like, "Do you know someone who's had an abortion?" and ask the people who do know someone to take a seat in the chairs. Then each one shares their personal experience.

It's interesting to watch the discussions because the tension between the groups at the beginning is palpable. But as each one shares their stories and personal experiences, you see empathy and understanding soften their faces. Rarely do people change the side that they came in on, but there is definitely a decrease in polarization—just from having a discussion with others—and looking each other in the eye.

While it's not always possible to have such a structured and facilitated dialogue with people you don't agree with, these videos illustrate how powerful it can be.[69]

Help Create a New Story & Tell It

Americans have long told ourselves stories about our country. Think about it: free from sea to shining sea; the land of opportunity; a giant melting pot; a nation of laws, not of men; your land and my land. These stories have begun to fade away, and according to Harvard historian, Jill Lepore, in her new book, *This America*:

> *Nations, to make sense of themselves, need some kind of agreed-upon past. They can get it from scholars or they can get it from demagogues, but get it they will.*[70]

One task of Agents for Change is to create a new shared story for America that understands and honors differences.

There are stories that play into polarization in our society, and there are stories that help create unity. Polarizing stories come from a place of fear, lack, and limitation, whereas unifying stories come from a place of love, abundance, and peace.

Polarizing stories claim that one party is superior to the other, or that the other side is bad or evil. In polarizing stories, your group or hero is far superior to other groups and their supposed heroes.

Unifying stories, on the other hand, include those that create equality, find common ground, and understand the importance of working with others to find solutions.

In his article, "The Revolution Must Be Felt," Jeremy Flood writes:

Solidarity is a story. It's composed of our actions and our authenticity. It's about collective identity and collective struggle. We are not "stronger together" when half of us are "deplorable."

Flood is saying that we can't move forward in America—when half the people hate the other half. Agents for Change need to find ways to tell unifying stories that create a common ground and, an agreed-upon past, and remind us of the importance of working together to find solutions.[71]

Intentionally Frame Your Arguments

We'd like to think we are rational. However, research by Nobel Prize Winner Daniel Kahneman and Amos Tversky shows that it's simply not true. They found that we are consistently irrational. We have evolved as a species to rely on mental shortcuts that speed up our reasoning. This makes us very sensitive to how arguments are framed and what metaphors are used. In fact, in some contexts, this might have an even stronger effect on our reasoning than our own political views.

The way you frame a message may make it more or less difficult to find common ground. Framing your messages in a way that will appeal to a particular value system can appeal to their natural flow, creating a more meaningful dialogue.

In one study, Kahneman and Tversky described crime to half of a group as a "beast preying" on the city. For the other half, crime was described as a "virus infecting" the city. Just by changing the metaphor, they were able to influence people's beliefs about crime.

The people who heard the "preying beast" story were more likely to believe the crime deserved punishment. Those exposed to the "virus infection" metaphor were more likely to support reform of the criminal justice system instead, and saw crime as something that could be cured.

A remarkable thing was that none of the participants realized the metaphors influenced their opinions. When asked what impacted their decision, they only mentioned the crime statistics they'd been told about—they didn't acknowledge the metaphor or its effect.[72]

Let's try it. Which of the following backcountry rescue squads would you hope was on duty if you were lost in the woods?

Our rescue attempts are 96 percent successful.
Or
One of every 25 of our rescue attempts fail.

Most of us would say that the company with the 96 percent success rate is the most appealing, even though the outcome is exactly the same.

See how important it is to be conscious and intentional when your frame your arguments? If not, you may be reinforcing negative metaphors and potentially alienating those you're trying to help.

One of the best-known examples of this is when Richard Nixon gave his infamous, "I am not a crook" speech in November of 1973. He was trying to clear his name from the Watergate scandal, but his speech had the opposite effect. Our brains ignored the "not." So instead, he reinforced the idea for millions of Americans that he was indeed a "crook."

Frames are made up of elements as well as expectations for those elements. Take, for instance, a hospital. A hospital has doctors, surgeons, patients, and an x-ray machine, just to name a few of its elements. When you visit a friend who's in the hospital, you don't expect to be asked to perform surgery on a doctor. That would break the frame in our mind.[73]

One of the main things to remember about framing is not to use language from an opposing viewpoint. Their language ties to a frame— and it may not be the frame you want.

Here's an example: When George W. Bush was in the White House; he used the phrase "tax relief" multiple times. By using the term "relief," he tapped into our frame that someone is afflicted and he is helping them. When he put the word "tax" with "relief," he created a metaphor that taxes are an affliction, making him a hero for reducing them.

This metaphor caught on and soon it was on television and in the media. The Democrats responded by denouncing his "tax relief" plan by name, which only reinforced the metaphor and increased Bush's popularity.

George Lakeoff is a cognitive psychologist and linguist who provides insight into framing and the use of metaphors in his book, *Don't Think of an Elephant*. He writes,

> *Framing is about getting language that fits your worldview. It is not just language. The ideas are primary and the language carries those ideas, evokes those ideas.*[74]

How to Frame Change

When having a dialogue, reframing can help you connect to another person. First, identify the value system being used by the other person. In other words, what color are they expressing—Blue, Orange, Green, Yellow? Then, try to reframe your own views in a way that draws on their predominant value system.

To really understand another's perspective, you need to know why they feel the way they do. One color can look like another at first glance, it's only when you understand the "why" behind the belief that you can accurately connect to the color.

For example, someone may say, "I am against the death penalty." This individual may be Blue and may not believe in the death penalty because it's against one of the 10 Commandments, "Thou shalt not kill." Or they're Orange and don't believe in the death penalty because research shows it's ineffective as a deterrent. Of course, this example is a little extreme but it helps you see that the motivations behind statements are key to understanding.

The purpose of framing is to help find common ground, not to change someone's belief. You can't "explain" someone from one layer into another.

If you are able to reframe and show them how your position connects to their underlying values, they will be much more receptive to it. Even if they don't agree with you, you'll increase understanding on a particular issue and be more likely to find mutual solutions.

Engaging All Colors to Combat Climate Change

One example of framing is the discussion of climate change. If you're trying to increase recycling, you would frame your argument differently depending on your audience. The message and goals don't change, only the framing.

So, if you were presenting to a Blue religious organization that doesn't believe in climate change, rather than focusing on climate change, you could focus your argument around the need to be a good steward of our planet's resources.

If you were presenting to an Orange corporation, you could focus on the money they will get back from recycling, the improved employee morale (thus reducing turnover) by demonstrating care for the planet, and how these practices would appeal to their current and future customers.

Navigating Polarization in Social Media

Ok, let's talk about the elephant in the room. Social media is an enormous contributor to the cycle of polarization we are seeing in our society. People share memes and articles with "clickable" headlines that reflect only one perspective.

You "like" or "share" the things and people you agree with. Facebook uses this information to show you more of what you like. Over time, your feed fills up with articles and opinions that you support, and very few that you don't.

If you happen to check the comments, you'll see they get heated very quickly. It makes for a contentious environment but does not allow for a real discussion about why someone feels the way they do, all the factors that should be considered, or the sources for credible information. No one wants to be attacked, so you're less likely to engage with posts you disagree with, and certainly less likely to have a meaningful conversation.

Your feed becomes an echo chamber where you only see opinions that support your own, whether they are accurate or not. You don't see articles or posts that create a productive dialogue that causes you to reflect on your own values and opinions. What are you missing? What are the other perspectives on this topic and what are their merits? Virtually all arguments have some merit.

Also, sites like Facebook and Google weren't originally designed to verify the information that is posted or indexed through their sites. Now, with the increase of paid advertising on the sites, they are encouraging us to prefer certain products and services, not just highlighting the things we already like. Whether we want to admit it or not, social media is changing our thoughts and preferences.

So, what can we do in the age of social media to combat polarization? Here are a few ideas:

1. **Follow the Common Ground Guidelines from Earlier in this Chapter.** Above all, always be respectful.

2. **Get Clear on Your Intentions.** Before liking, sharing, or posting anything, ask yourself: what is my intention? Do I want to draw attention to a specific issue, generate action from my friends, or create an opportunity for open discussion? If the post is only aimed at virtue signaling (wanting people to know how cool, generous, or open-minded you are) or inflaming tensions, it might be better left unshared.

3. **Know Your Sources.** What is the source of the information? Be careful about sharing clickbait headlines that may not be based in truth or information from sites that only look at one perspective.

4. **Consider Other Perspectives.** Read or listen to information that you may not agree with initially in order to better understand the arguments on the other side.

5. **Research the Topic.** Read information from a range of sources and perspectives.

Social media can be polarizing and stressful, but it doesn't have to be. Some have been able to reclaim their social media feeds and cutting their "friend" lists to only close friends and family members. They continually "cull" their feed ensuring that the content they see is useful and inspiring. Others are limiting their time online or abandoning social media altogether to focus more on offline human connection.

Companies like Facebook and Twitter are also implementing new controls to reduce negative polarization on the sites.

While social media can be a useful tool for connecting with others, it was never designed for deep and meaningful conversations about complex and nuanced topics. In the same way you wouldn't start an intense discussion standing in the checkout line at your local grocery store, trying to have a conversation on social media is also not very effective. Short sound bites with someone you can't see or hear is a recipe for confusion and miscommunication.

In summary

If Nelson Mandela could find common ground in South Africa during apartheid, you can find it in your situation. Start with meaningful dialogue in a calm environment, with established ground rules. Listen and validate the other, sharing values and fears, and agree on a resource for checking facts when necessary. Be part of creating a new story for your community and the country. Learn to tell unifying stories and frame your arguments for most effectiveness. And remember, the goal is finding common ground, not changing someone's beliefs.

When communicating on social media, be respectful and mindful of your intentions. Research the topic, consider other perspectives, and be informed before you post. Whether you continue to use social media or not, the future will be determined by the relationships you build within your own community as we'll discuss in the next chapter.

CHAPTER 9

Building Resilient Communities

The way to change the world is through individual responsibility
and taking local action in your own community.

~JEFF BRIDGES

My friend Karen McNenny is an amazing speaker, social activist, and consultant. I thought the tagline she adopted many years ago—"Community is the CURE" was clever at the time, but I had no idea how right she was.

Karen is best known for her TED Talk, "How Shopping Cart Behavior Will Transform Society." It's about how seemingly small actions like putting your shopping cart away at the store will create more social engagement, and a kinder and more intentional society. Because, as you've probably heard, how you do *anything*, is how you do *everything*.[75]

In the last year, I have spent hundreds of hours looking for the best ways to reduce polarization in society. I hoped to find a magic bullet, something that would get results easily and quickly but that wasn't the case. I did, however, discover some amazing tools and resources, including The Change Code, that can help. I'll highlight these in the next chapter. What I found at the core, is that indeed, Community *is* the CURE.

Community is the cure for the extreme isolation and individualism that has taken over our society. It's the cure for the lack of kindness and empathy that has become the norm, especially in our online world. A strong sense of healthy community also helps as we journey through change and can help alleviate feelings of loneliness, distrust, and meaninglessness that are part of the Four "Interrelated Social Crises" I mentioned earlier.

And, it's the cure for easing the chaos, fear, and uncertainty we are feeling as we transition from the Orange layer to the Green layer as a society.

It turns out that neighborhoods and communities are the unit for change. While it's nice to help individuals, the real difference comes when you help an entire neighborhood.

In *The Second Mountain*, David Brooks shares the example of a swimming pool. You can't just clean one corner of the pool, you have to clean the whole pool to create change. This kind of change is possible at the neighborhood and community level.[76]

Your community helps determine your health, how long you live, whether you are safe and secure, your financial status, and how likely it is that your children will succeed. Creating positive change for even one community has a tremendous ripple effect for the local residents, their children, extended family members, the state, and even the nation.

You might not be able to change lives on the other side of the world, but you can take on something small in our own community. In *The Abundant Community*, John McKnight and Peter Block describe the "Seven Elements of Satisfaction" for an abundant community:

1. **Our neighborhoods are the primary source of our health.** The elements for wellness come from our personal behaviors, our environment, and our income. These are things we can impact when we work together with our neighbors.

Agents for Change:
Eliminating Heart Disease in
Southwest Minnesota

The residents of New Ulm, Minnesota, worked with their local hospital to reduce heart attacks in their community. The Heart of New Ulm is a 10-year program backed by a one-million-dollar annual investment to address the social determinants of health related to heart attacks. These are things like diet, exercise, and social connection, which make up 80 percent of the risk for heart-attack patients.

People in the community pulled together to improve menus at local restaurants, create opportunities for exercise, and support vulnerable residents. The local hospital collaborated with other community organizations, employers, and non-profits to engage them in the process as well.

The program has been highly successful at reducing heart attacks, hypertension, diabetes, and smoking in the community, while also improving physical activity, nutrition, and increasing connection.[77]

2.   **Our safety and security are also tied to community.** There are two major determinants for safety, one is how many neighbors

we know by name, and the second is how often we are present and engaged in public—getting out of our homes.

3. **The environment is a local responsibility.** While some environmental issues feel beyond our control, *we* can control our transportation choices, how we heat our homes, and how much waste we create.

4. **We have the power to build a resilient economy.** Most enterprises begin locally, in someone's home or garage. We have the power to nurture and support local businesses, preserve our own savings, and help neighbors in their job search. We can create more security in our local economy.

5. **The food we eat matters.** We can support local food producers and markets. This helps reduce energy consumption, improves the local economy, and increases our access to healthy foods free of toxic pesticides and processing. All of this improves our overall health.

Agents for Change in a Small Nebraska Town

The residents of the rural Midwest community of Cody, Nebraska, wanted to provide access to healthy food for the entire 550-mile sparsely populated district that is home to 480 people. Cody is considered a "food desert" or an area with limited access to healthy food as measured by distance to a store. In this case, a grocery store is more than an hour away. Residents created the local Circle C Market, a non-profit grocery store run by volunteers and area high-school students who stock shelves.

The business teacher at the high school oversees the store in addition to her teaching duties. Students earn a paycheck for hours worked, as well as academic credit hours and learn hands-on business and people skills. The community supports the market by shopping there and residents help out when they can. In return, the market buys meat and produce from local suppliers whenever possible.[78]

6. **We raise our children locally.** Our communities can become villages of support for youth. After all, a youth problem is a community problem, and is one we can address. Just like the story of Nunpa and his work to create AntFarm, one person can make a difference.

7. **Our communities are the site for care.** Care is the "freely given commitment from the heart of one to another" and it cannot be purchased. As neighbors, we can care for each other, our children, our elders, and our most vulnerable."[79]

Agents for Change in
My Own Neighborhood

I've witnessed the power of community on my own street, and the impact that one person can have by making a commitment to creating community. I've lived in many neighborhoods over the years, but none as welcoming as the one where I live now. In most places I've lived (including in small towns), the neighbors barely know each other and never interacted.

Within a few days of moving into this house, however, our next-door neighbor Sena welcomed us with a small bag of chocolates and a friendly smile. When we see her outside, she makes a point to say hello and ask how we're doing. She introduced us to other neighbors and always offers to lend a hand. When we travel, she has walked our dogs, and gotten our mail. When a neighbor is sick, she brings them soup. As a result of her connection, we are closer to our other neighbors as well and support them when they need it and they support us. Our neighborhood is a true community. It feels safe and secure to know that those around us keep an eye out for us.

We have the ability to create positive change when we start at the community level.

Community and the Colors

From The Change Code, we know we are emerging from the Orange layer as a society. The next stage of development is Green which is a *communal* layer. The Green layer takes the focus off material success and puts it on healing the self and the planet and bringing people back together.

As an Agent for Change, your job is to find ways to bring back a sense of belonging and community, uniting people from all backgrounds and value systems, creating a culture and environment where individuals care about each other and their neighbors.

One way to find solutions is to look at what worked in earlier communal layers. With Blue, religion was a primary focus, as were rules and social norms. With Purple, family was the primary focus.

In the Green layer, elements of Blue and Purple will return, only at a higher octave (a more complex layer on the spiral of development). So, we may again turn to some of the rituals from religion, for example, gathering together on certain days, incorporating rituals, songs, chants, and spiritual connection. These rituals have been used for thousands of years to connect people and have actually been shown to provide health benefits. That doesn't necessarily mean a return to formalized religion—although some may choose that path, but we will find new ways to bring these elements into our communities.

In his book, *Science and Spiritual Practices*, Rupert Sheldrake reviews seven kinds of practices and their scientific benefits including singing and chanting, the practices of gratitude, meditation, spirituality and connecting with the "more-than-human" world, relating to plants, rituals and rites of passage, and pilgrimages to holy places.

We may also see a resurgence of existing community-service organizations, along with new ones. The Green value system has a need for deep connection, so strategies that facilitate this connection will be valuable and important. As an Agent for Change, you can help create these connections.

Horizons – A Personal Example
of Facilitating Change

Early in my career, I participated in a facilitative leadership process called Horizons in my small Montana community. The goal was to address the growing concern of rural poverty in the state.

Upon completion of the program, the town would receive a $1,000 grant toward a project that we would develop. The 18-month program had four phases: community conversations about poverty, leadership training and visioning, community visioning and planning, and idea implementation.

Horizons welcomed input from participants on how we could improve our community. We met in large groups for a free spaghetti dinner, and then broke up into smaller groups. I led one of the smaller groups for a number of weeks. We talked about what was and wasn't working. We got creative and brainstormed possible solutions.

At another spaghetti dinner, everyone shared their ideas on large pieces of paper. Each person then voted by placing a sticky note next to their favorite ideas for change.

The exact idea that won the grant money is irrelevant. The point is that once the community came together to discuss challenges *and* solutions, people got excited and saw tangible ways they could contribute to their community. And the spirit of change trickled down: Inspired individuals stepped in to do many smaller, informal projects. As a result, our town gained a new walking path along the river, a sign board by the only grocery store for important announcements and upcoming events, and a community bulletin board.

As participants got to know each other better and made new friends, there was an improved sense of community that's still in place today. That experience always stayed with me, as did the lesson of the power of bringing people together in a collaborative partnership.

What would a process like this look like in your neighborhood or community?[80]

In summary

Community is the cure. Creating positive change in your community has a ripple effect from residents, to their children, the state, and even the nation. Issues concerning health, environment, economics, food, safety, youth and resiliency are all local issues. And as an Agent for Change you can help create community connections and feelings of belonging.

Now I get to share with you some of the most amazing, game-changing tools I have discovered in my research.

CHAPTER 10

Game-Changing Tools for Changemakers

No more awards for forecasting the rain,
Only for building the ark.
~DR. DON BECK

Remember Wicked Problems? Those tough problems that can't be "solved" the way we've historically done but must be continually navigated? This is because everything is interconnected, and one "solution" creates new problems. For instance, poverty is a problem that's linked to education, nutrition, the economy, etc., so every possible solution for poverty has ramifications in those areas. Working through Wicked Problems is not easy—it requires collaboration and diverse perspectives.

Easy to say, I know. So how do we do that?

In this chapter, I'll tell you about three tools you want to have at the ready that are *invaluable* for creating and implementing change: Polarity Mapping & Management®, Appreciative Inquiry, and Deliberative Engagement.

One thing about Wicked Problems is they are packed full of polarities which we discussed in Chapter 1. A polarity means there are two sides to an issue. Each side of the polarity is interdependent, which means if you choose one side, you will neglect the other. If you can picture a pendulum swinging between two opposing sides, it is likely a polarity.

Polarity Mapping®

Welcome to Polarity Mapping®, a simple yet highly effective technique for understanding other perspectives, identifying the limitations of an approach, getting everyone on the same page, and developing workable solutions, even if you have a problem that doesn't seem to be solvable. It has many applications and can be easily used to help facilitate discussions. The technique was developed by Dr. Barry Johnson and has been used by Fortune 100 companies, the U.S. Department of Defense, universities, consultants, non-profits, and individuals. When I discovered it, I was blown away by both the simplicity of it—and at the way it can help groups navigate Wicked Problems.

The map provides a structure for making invisible tensions visible and for addressing the whole polarity picture. Once a group completes the map through collaborative conversation, it provides a focus for them to discuss issues from diverse perspectives. Then, groups and leaders can use the map to actively identify ongoing action steps to navigate the positive attributes of each pole, while monitoring for the early warning signs of negative results.

A Polarity Map® consists of four quadrants. On the left is one polarity and on the right is the other side of that polarity. The top two quadrants are the upside for each side of the polarity. The bottom two quadrants are the downsides.

Once they've mapped a polarity, the group can work together to identify ways for staying in the upsides of both poles, creating harmony—while avoiding the downsides.

There are six steps for mapping a polarity.

POLARITY MAP

Action Steps

How will we gain or maintain the positive results from focusing on this left pole? What? Who? By When? Measures?

Enter "Action Steps:"

Action Steps

How will we gain or maintain the positive results from focusing on this right pole? What? Who? By When? Measures?

Enter "Action Steps:"

General Purpose Statement (GPS) - Why leverage this polarity?
Enter "GPS"

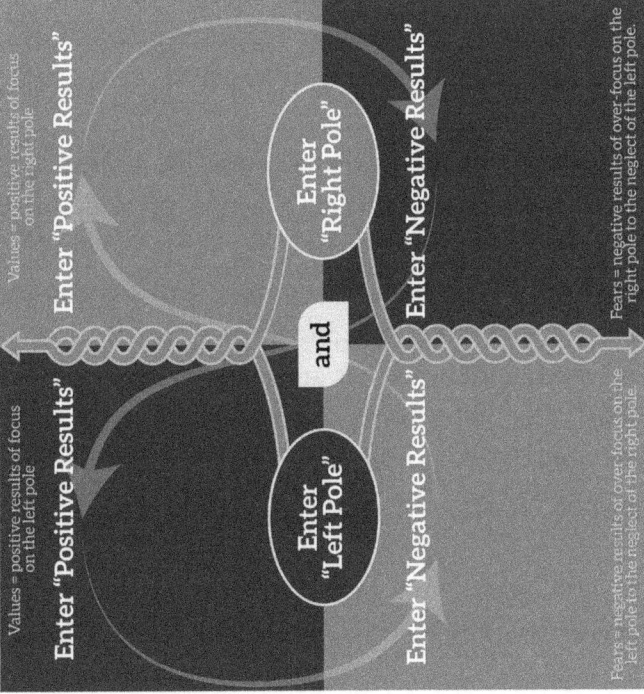

Values = positive results of focus on the left pole

Enter "Positive Results"

Values = positive results of focus on the right pole

Enter "Positive Results"

Enter "Left Pole"

and

Enter "Right Pole"

Enter "Negative Results"

Enter "Negative Results"

Fears = negative results of over-focus on the left pole to the neglect of the right pole.

Fears = negative results of over-focus on the right pole to the neglect of the left pole.

Enter "Deeper Fear"
Deeper Fear - Loss of GPS

Early Warnings

Measurable indicators (things you can count) that will let you know that you are getting into the downside of this left pole.

Enter "Early Warnings:"

Early Warnings

Measurable indicators (things you can count) that will let you know that you are getting into the downside of this right pole.

Enter "Early Warnings:"

1. **Confirm that you have a polarity.** Once you've confirmed that you have a polarity in a problem you are trying to address, discuss the issues in a way that doesn't place blame on others and create a description of the problem.

    • Examples of polarities include: Change/Stay the Same, Centralize/Decentralize, Short-term/Long-term

2. **Agree on the names for the poles.** These names should be value-neutral. For example, names like Ray's Great Plan and Joe's Stupid Plan would not be neutral.

3. **Write the pole names on the map.** The entire group should be able to see the map as it unfolds during the discussion.

4. **Brainstorm together the content for each quadrant.** Try to come up with four to eight entries for each quadrant. You can ask the question, "What are some positives or upsides of this pole?" The brainstorming process helps the group understand the complexity of the issue and the face that each side has positive aspects.

    For example, if your organization is considering purchasing a new software system, you might look at the polarities of buying the software or staying with the manual system. For instance, the software will help you become more efficient and accurate. It will also allow you to serve more customers without hiring more employees.

    But, you may lose some of the personal interaction with customers because you're looking at the computer screen. The software is also expensive and has maintenance fees.

5. **Agree on a higher purpose and a deeper fear.** When the group agrees on these, they have a reason to manage the tension between the two views. They see the full picture. The higher purpose is the major benefit for managing the polarity while the deeper fear is the major negative for not managing the polarity well. In the previous example, the higher purpose is improving the long-term sustainability of the organization and the deeper fear is losing jobs and customers.

6. **Develop action steps and identify early warning signs.** Action steps will maintain positive results and flag early warning signs so you know that you are moving into the downsides of the poles.[81] For instance, your company may monitor customer feedback to see if customer service has been affected by the new software.

Let's look at another example. Imagine your tomato-sauce business is considering implementing a new type of sustainable food storage material and using that as a differentiator in the marketplace. Some members of your team are excited to make this change, but others think it's too risky. The new packaging costs more and degrades faster. The selling process would have to be faster too. They'd rather keep things the same.

Taking them through a Polarity Mapping® process helps everyone see both sides of this polarity and find a way to balance the needs between the two. Then, they can use the map to move forward with positive steps and have a sense of what to avoid. Instead of an either/or solution that we know won't work, the Polarity Map® can facilitate a way to continually navigate and monitor the many aspects of a polarized Wicked Problem.

POLARITY MAPPING®:
STAY THE SAME OR CHANGE

Greater Purpose Statement (GPS) - Why leverage this polarity?
Organization brings the best of it's past and present into its desired future.

Action Steps

How will we gain or maintain the positive results from focusing on this left pole?
What? Who? By When? Measures?

Action Steps

How will we gain or maintain the positive results from focusing on this right pole?
What? Who? By When? Measures?

Values = positive results of focus on the left pole

Desire to Stay the Same

A. We value the tried and true solutions we've been using
B. We have clear and/or understood ways of getting our work done
C. We hold on to business processes that we are confident will support us in achieving our current and future needs

and

Values = positive results of focus on the right pole

Desire to Change

A. We welcome solutions that keep us on the leading edge
B. We are open to new and/or improved ways of working
C. Our drive to adopt best practice processes is grounded in the realities of our current and future business needs

Early Warnings

Measurable indicators (things you can count) that will let you know that you are getting into the downside of this left pole.

Early Warnings

Measurable indicators (things you can count) that will let you know that you are getting into the downside of this right pole.

Fears = negative results of over-focus on the right pole to the neglect of the left pole.

A. We are generally resistant to the idea of change
B. We are stuck in old ways of working that no longer serve us
C. We fail to improve our business processes even when we know they no longer meet our current and/or future needs

Running in Place

Deeper Fear resulting from a failure to leverage this Polarity

A. Suggested best practice solutions fail to meet our business needs
B. We are unclear about how work should be done
C. We are so focused on change that we fail to recognize when the way we are doing things is a best practice

Fears = negative results of over-focus on the left pole to the neglect of the right pole.

In this example, the polarities are, "Desire to Stay the Same" and "Desire to Change". This map would work for most types of change within an organization.

There are positive results from staying the same, including feeling confident about current processes. There are also positive results from changing, including looking at solutions that will keep the business on the leading edge.

There are also negative results from staying the same, including getting stuck in old ways that no longer serve. And, negative results from changing, including having staff members who are unclear about how work should get done.

After reviewing the Polarity Map®, this group determined that their ultimate goal, or Greater Purpose Statement (GPS) is to create an organization that brings the best of its past and present into its desired future.

You likely have encountered/are navigating such a polarity in your workplace, community, and in your personal life. Finding a balance between the polarities prevents the need for dramatic swings of the pendulum to autocorrect the imbalances.

For example, if your community is thinking about opening a new homeless shelter, there will be supporters for the idea as well as individuals who are against it. Supporters want to help the homeless. People who are opposed may live near the site of the shelter and be concerned about maintaining the safety of their neighborhood. Working together, there may be solutions to open the shelter AND maintain safety in the neighborhood by creating a neighborhood watch program, providing more patrols, and ensuring adequate staffing and resources at the shelter.

Once the Polarity Map® has been completed, the work isn't finished, however. Polarity Management® is the active management of the issue that will help prevent the group from slipping too far in any direction. Part of this active management is observing tensions in conversations and listening for complaints.

For example, the Executive Director for that new homeless shelter would track petty crimes in the neighborhood, as well as complaints or feedback from residents. If she sees an increase, she knows they need to look at their active solutions. She is proactive in addressing changes in the neighborhood and brings key stakeholders back for discussions as needed.

Because the polarities in our Wicked Problems are never fully solved, this tool helps us create "good-enough-for-now" solutions that we can manage and revisit as needed to adjust our approach. This ongoing polarity management is what will be needed for individuals, organizations, and governments in the future.

Appreciative Inquiry

Another one of my favorite tools for change is Appreciative Inquiry. It is based on the premise that humans—societies, groups, and individuals—move in the direction of what they focus on, and asking the right questions is key to understanding what you value and appreciate. It helps you create a compelling vision for the future with a design that is based on your strengths.[82]

The questions you ask determine the answers you will receive, the actions you will take, and the outcomes you will achieve. The types of questions you ask are extremely powerful in determining where you and your organization will go. Questions should be genuine and not leading or Socratic. In our time of complexity, being open to new information, data, and novel solutions will give you an advantage.

Certain questions will engage your very linear, problem-solving left brain: Why is this system so broken? Whose fault is this? What bad things will happen if…? These are questions coming from a scarcity mindset. A scarcity mindset looks at the world as full of threats and not having enough for everyone.

Other questions get your creative right brain going: What is possible with this system? How would your ideal system look and feel? What is another way to look at this problem? What is the very best move you can make? These questions come from an abundance mindset. An abundance mindset views the world as being full of opportunity and having enough for everyone.[83]

Imagine being asked the question, "Why is there so much poverty in our community?" This question engages the left side of your brain and moves you into problem-solving mode.

How would you answer this question?

You might bring up the high unemployment rate, the cost of housing, childcare, cost of living, lack of education and training, mental health issues, lack of healthcare—the list could go on and on and seem pretty dismal. You'd start to feel the weight of the world on your shoulders again. Where do you even begin?

However, when you use an Appreciative Inquiry approach, you ask a different question, like: "How do we create a community where everyone's basic needs are met?"

Wow, what a difference, right? The Appreciative Inquiry question engages the right side of your brain and taps into creativity, vision, and intuition.

How would you answer *this* question?

You might start dreaming of things like building affordable housing, community centers with affordable kids' activities for children to support working parents, providing training on ways to start a side business, and more.

Notice how different that feels energetically than a long list of problems. Pretty good, eh? Congratulations— you've actually created a long list of possible *solutions*.

The systems for the future will come from a creative, intuitive, right-brain perspective like this, working in tandem with left-brain problem solving and technical skills. And Appreciative Inquiry is an amazing tool to facilitate that process.

The answers for systems for the future will come from a creative, intuitive, right-brain perspective working in tandem with left-brain problem solving and technical skills. Appreciative Inquiry is a useful tool to help facilitate that process.

Deliberative Engagement

One of the problems with our current legislative process is that by the time people are asked for input on a specific issue, it's presented in a polarizing way—yes or no. People feel like they have to take one side or the other and need to vote that way.

And remember, politicians are generally more extreme than the people they represent. So the legislative process further increases this polarity, and ignores all of the nuances around complex issues.

Enter Deliberative Engagement. This process helps navigate these problems by creating a mutual understanding and genuine interaction between polarized sides. Instead of looking for a magic bullet or someone to villainize, Deliberative Engagement also helps to create "good-enough-for-now" solutions that we can adjust as we learn more and circumstances change. It is especially effective for communities wrangling with Wicked Problems on a local level, as well as for groups and organization.

The process of Deliberative Engagement creates more optimal solutions because it brings together diverse perspectives to work through the often messy and potentially polarizing nuances of an issue.

The solutions from Deliberative Engagement often require the group to adapt to the changing landscape. If a community is discussing a water shortage, for instance, homeowners may need to adapt to limited times for watering lawns rather than watering any time they choose.

Optimal solutions from this process often include multiple levels in society, including public policy at the national, state, and local levels. They require the community to get involved and organizations and social institutions to collaborate and also require individuals to increase their knowledge, improve their skills, and change their attitudes.[84]

The Four Stages of Deliberative Engagement:

- **Divergent Thinking**. Deliberative engagement brings together individuals with diverse perspectives early in the discussions. Whether it's via public or group comment, focus groups, email, or surveys. The goal is to identify differences in opinions and to avoid the mistake of believing there is a consensus when there is not.

- **Working Through "the Groan Zone."** Once you've identified all the opinions, you use facilitated, structured dialogue and deliberation or small group discussions to work through the inevitable gripes and complaints. This process, which can be laborious (hence "groan"), and helps participants look at the different value systems and beliefs at play, along with the complexity of the problem, to hopefully form a better understanding of all the consequences that could result from any one decision.

- **Convergent Thinking**. Once the group is through the "Groan Zone", you are able to move into Action Mode—prioritization, innovation, and collaborative planning.[85]

It's important to note that Deliberative Engagement is not a quick process, but it can create lasting positive results. Some communities have worked through the various stages in two to six months or more. Through this process however, groups within the community feel like their voices are heard and like they've been part of the process. It requires compromise all around but strengthens the community as a whole.

In summary

Agents for Change are all the more powerful when they use proven tools. Polarity Mapping® helps groups and organizations move forward when they are navigating polarized situations. Appreciative Inquiry's beautiful method of questioning opens up possibility instead of creating defensiveness. And Deliberative Engagement helps groups facing divergent thinking to step into action.

OK, that's it for me and what I'm passionate about. Now it's time for you. In the next chapter, we'll look at what matters to you and what you're ready to commit to.

CHAPTER 11

Committing to Change

*Choose your corner, pick away at it carefully, intensely and
to the best of your ability and that way you might change the world.*
~CHARLES EAMES

So now you know the Theory of Everything, but what are you going
to do when you get out of bed tomorrow morning?

I recently had dinner with my colleague Todd. We were discussing
polarization and the challenges we see right now. (Yes, this is the stuff I
love to talk about over dinner.) Even though Todd works in healthcare
and makes a positive difference every day, he said, "I can pretend that
liking or sharing an article on Facebook makes me an activist, but it
doesn't do anything at all. I deleted my Facebook account and want to
do something that actually matters! But where do I even begin?"

Maybe you feel like Todd—overwhelmed or frustrated by everything that's happening, and not sure what to do. You're not alone.
This is fight or flight mode and when we're in that state, it's hard to
see solutions.

I'm proud of Todd and even though he might not call himself one,
he's an Agent for Change. While he's not exactly sure what's next, he's
moving into that space of uncertainty and feeling his way through it.
It's not easy and sometimes it can be scary— knowing you're meant to
do more and reaching into the unknown to explore the possibilities.

We're stuck in the middle of two worlds, the chaotic current-day reality of society on the one hand and our own personal microcosm on the other. It's like we have one foot on the dock and another on the boat, and the boat's beginning to drift away. We know we're supposed to do something, to do more, and that there must be a better way. We're just not sure what that looks like.

I believe that's why you're here right now, on this planet. Your vision, leadership, and quite frankly, your *light* are needed now more than ever. You are one of the pathfinders, helping to find the openings for creating what's next, helping others through the chaos, or just spreading kindness and compassion.

This conversation with Rob got me thinking. Where can someone begin if they know they want to make a difference but aren't sure where to start?

When I interviewed Nunpa at AntFarm (Chapter 7), I started thinking about how much difference one person can make by just committing to something. When he started AntFarm more than six years ago, there were limited programs and resources to help the youth in the community. And the building was just an abandoned plumbing store.

Since then, AntFarm has served more than 1000 youth and 600+ seniors while employing more than 300 people. That's a mighty impact that came from Nunpa's decision and his commitment to see it through.

When I last spoke to Nunpa, I asked him what advice he would give to someone who wanted to create positive change but wasn't sure where to begin. He told me:

> *Just start. Whether it's finding a local non-profit or a church where you can volunteer or by reaching out and helping an elderly neighbor, just start. And don't underestimate the importance of being kind to others and smiling.*

He said people get too hung up in the paralysis of fear—not sure they can do it and worrying about every small detail—but you won't know until you give it a try. You are capable of far more than you know. You just need to step into that fear over and over again, because it never goes away.

Not everyone wants to or is able to commit to creating and leading a non-profit organization. That takes a big commitment. For Nunpa, it's a commitment for life, leading Ant Farm is what he's here to do.

So where do *you* start?

It's important to think about what causes you are passionate about as well as your level and ability to make a commitment. If you feel like you're already too busy with day-to-day living to take on a big project, there are still acts that only require a small commitment. I believe that everyone can do something, regardless of their circumstances. If you're not sure what you're passionate about, consider trying Michael Bernard Beckwith's Life Visioning Process. I mentioned it earlier in the book as well because it's had such an impact on my own life. (Find information in Resources.)

EXERCISE: What Are You Passionate About?

What causes are you most passionate about? Identifying these causes is your starting point. It's much easier to make a commitment to work toward something you believe in fully.

It's also important for you to identify the areas where you have a natural interest and passion. These areas may or may not be the same as the work you do to earn an income. To maintain the level of effort and commitment that change and development will take, tapping into your passion for a cause is what will keep you motivated and making progress.

So, what causes do you really care about? Start by making a list of as many things as you can think of.

animal welfare

the environment

reducing plastic use

arts for children

homelessness

equality

Once you've completed your list, see if you can narrow it down to your top 3-5 causes. Now circle one that you'd most like to start with.

About Commitment

The size of your commitment isn't the only thing that determines the impact of your actions. For example, you might make a commitment to smiling and being kind to others, including strangers, throughout your day. Your kind word may be enough to turn someone's day around. You simply don't know the full effect of your actions, either positive or negative. Your actions spur a chain reaction that carry far beyond the immediate moment.

For complex systems, of which we're all apart, there's a theory called the Butterfly Effect. It's defined as *"the sensitive dependence on initial conditions in which a small change in one state of a deterministic nonlinear system can result in large differences in a later state."*

To put it more simply, even the slightest change in one area can spark a large change in the whole.[86]

The phrase "Butterfly Effect" came from a talk given by Edward Lorenz in 1972, entitled, "Does the Flap of a Butterfly's Wings in Brazil Set Off a Tornado in Texas?" Although a butterfly flapping its wings is often used to describe this concept, the location of the butterfly, the consequences, and the location of the consequences have varied widely as it's been retold over the years.[87]

Lorenz is best known as the founder of modern chaos theory, resulting from his research into modern climate systems. He was quite possibly at Yellow based on his sophisticated work with chaotic systems and pattern recognition, although it's difficult to know without talking to him.[88]

The point to remember is this: no act is too small. You can make a difference and you can begin today.

Grab a blank piece of paper and just take a moment to think about what things you could do around the cause you chose that wouldn't require a lot of commitment, a few things that would require a little more commitment, and maybe one or two things that would require a major commitment, understanding that this last category may take a long time to complete. That's ok—you're just brainstorming.

1. Small Commitment
2. Medium Commitment
3. Major Commitment

For one person, helping an elderly neighbor carry in her groceries might be a small commitment, while for someone who struggles physically themselves or is super-busy, it might be a medium commitment. Find actions that are the right fit for you and that don't overburden you. When you feel overburdened, you're really not helping anyone.

Here are some ideas to get you started:

Small Commitment

John Paul Flintoff works to help protect the environment and prevent global warming. In his 2012 TED Talk, "How to Change the World," he talked about how you can actually make the greatest impact in your own backyard. He realized he could make an immediate difference by reaching out to his neighbors. However, he did it not by overloading them with facts and research, but by giving them tomato plants. Every year, he offers his extra tomato seedlings to his neighbors. This simple and kind act inspired his neighbors to start growing some of their own food, thereby slightly reducing their environmental impact. [89]

What's something you can do in your own backyard?

Dream Big, Start Small

Start small and just take the first step. This was the secret of Nobel Prize winner Muhammad Yunus, the pioneer of microfinance and microlending. Before he retired, Yunus helped thousands of people in poverty obtain business loans without collateral. He started with just $27.

Yunus surveyed people in his community about their needs, and was shocked to learn that he could assist 42 people by lending just $27 of his own money. His first project was a success and he continued to build on it, eventually creating Grameen Bank. By 1997, Grameen Bank had issued US$6.38 billion to 7.4 million borrowers, empowering others to build businesses and improve their own situations. Yunus went on to successfully lead several other initiatives to help the poor, starting small each time.

Sometimes a small commitment might just mean starting small but having a bigger vision for what you might accomplish. You don't have to take on everything at once, in fact, it's better if you don't.

Shop Wisely

Another way to start small is to limit your spending to businesses that share your values and that have positive business practices—including fair trade and a triple bottom line of "people, planet, and profit" (not just profit). Take the time to learn about the companies where you do business. Does your bank use ethical business practices? What types of projects do they fund? What goes into making your favorite latte at the coffee shop? How about your cosmetics? What companies are included in the investments for your 401k?

Let your money make a statement. While it may not seem like a lot, if enough people redirect their spending based on unethical or unsustainable practices, businesses will change and evolve to meet the demand. If you spend according to your own values, you'll not only make a statement, you'll also find more harmony with your money.

Make a list of the products and services you buy most. Do their business practices align with your values? If not, what are your other options?

Practice Random Acts of Kindness

Think of the last time someone paused to let you merge into their lane on the highway, sent you an unexpected card in the mail, or gave you a smile on the street. How good did *that* feel? Maybe it changed your whole outlook. A small act of kindness creates a ripple effect that can carry from person to person, brightening many lives. It doesn't take a lot to make someone's day a little bit brighter.

Research has also found that performing these simple acts of kindness increases feelings of happiness and positivity. One study even found that:

> *Acts of kindness create an emotional warmth, which releases a hormone known as oxytocin. Oxytocin causes the release of a chemical called nitric oxide, which dilates the blood vessels. This reduces blood pressure and, therefore, oxytocin is known as a "cardioprotective" hormone. It protects the heart by lowering blood pressure.*

My friend Clint used to buy coffee for the people in the car behind him at the drive-through. He's since passed away, but he received immense joy from knowing he just gave someone a nice surprise and had no expectation of anything in return.

I've done this myself a few times and it's fun to imagine the surprise for the person in the car behind me. I've also had someone unexpectedly do the same for me, and it came as a real shock. I was speechless. I sent that person feelings of gratitude that I know extended out to those directly around me for the rest of the day.

> I alone cannot change the world, but I can cast a stone across the waters to create many ripples.
>
> —*Mother Teresa*

One of the small-commitment things I've done for years is save all those sample-sized soaps and shampoos from hotel bathrooms. I travel a fair amount for work, so these add up quickly. I put them in a box when I get home and then a few times per year, I take the box to our local women's shelter for use in their shower facilities.

This action only takes a few minutes after each trip and about an hour to drop off the box, and it costs me no money. Yet, I know the women in the shelter who feel fresh and clean after a shower are in a better place, even if only for a little while.

Medium Commitment

A medium commitment is something that requires more time, energy, and possibly investment than a small commitment, but isn't as time or energy-consuming as a major commitment.

Some examples might include volunteering once a week at your church or a local homeless shelter, or leading a food drive for the county animal shelter. Maybe it's writing a book, or handling the social media for a local non-profit.

One of the most enjoyable medium commitments I've made was to lead my daughter's Girl Scout troop when she was in fourth and fifth grades. It took a fair amount of time to organize weekly activities, cookie sales, and field trips for a troop of 30 girls, but it was a great way to spend quality time with my daughter, and make a positive impact on girls in her school. We went camping, learned basic survival skills, and saw a lot of great speakers and role models from the community, including a female police officer.

What are some medium commitments that you might want to try?

Major Commitment

A major commitment is something that requires a *lot* of time to complete and may involve some risk or investment on your part.

When I think of major commitment, I think of Nunpa leaving his full-time job to launch AntFarm, not knowing for certain that he would be able to support himself or make it sustainable.

It's that commitment that allows him to go to the bakery in the middle of the night to clean up floodwater from a massive rainstorm. Or, when one of his employees quit unexpectedly, water all the city's flower pots himself at 4:00 am for an entire summer to keep an agreement with the community.

When I asked Nunpa if he ever feels overwhelmed or burdened by all that he's taken on, he said, "No, I have times where I get tired or feel strong emotions, just like everybody else, but I don't feel burdened by the work. I just know that it's what I'm here to do and that feels really good." Ideally, that's what our major commitments should feel like.

I also think of Dr. Don Beck who used his retirement savings to work with Nelson Mandela in South Africa and help prevent a civil war. He then went on to spend the rest of his life teaching and mentoring others, including me, about Spiral Dynamics. This was a *major* commitment for Dr. Beck, his wife, and his entire family. Does he regret it? Not one bit. Now in his 80s, he feels like he's had a rich life full of amazing experiences. And, he's not finished, he still speaks, writes, and supports new initiatives when possible.

Sometimes something that starts off as a small or medium commitment may grow into a major commitment, just like Muhammad Yunus and Grameen Bank. Trying to start a bank with $6 billion dollars would have felt overwhelming and unattainable at the beginning. Yunus started where he was, with $27, and the program blossomed into an enormous organization benefitting people all over the world.

Do you want to make a major commitment but aren't sure where to start? Here are two questions to consider:

1. **What would you do if you knew you wouldn't fail?**
   This question helps you think big without the doubt or negative self-talk. I recently posed this question to my Facebook community and some of the answers I got back included curing AIDS, eradicating malaria, working with DNA to prevent illness, and writing a best-selling novel. What beautiful goals. Dream big — what would you do?

2. **What is one thing you can start doing toward that goal within the next 24 hours?**
   Big goals can be daunting, but focusing on only the next action allows you to make progress without feeling overwhelmed. Don't wait—begin with just one small step and keep it up. Before you know it, you'll have moved mountains.[90]

Daily Practice

Making a commitment and keeping it can sometimes be two different things. Once you've decided where to commit your time and energy, a good exercise is setting your intentions daily. I learned this great exercise from Joshua Becker of the Becoming Minimalist blog and love to do as part of my morning yoga routine.[91]

Each day you complete this sentence:

"Today, I commit myself to_____ ."

You get to fill in the blank every morning, in any way you choose. For example,

- Today, I commit to being the best wife and mother I can be.
- Today, I commit to being kind to everyone I encounter.
- Today, I commit to my own mindfulness, self-care, and personal development.
- Today, I commit to taking at least one action toward my bigger goals.
- Today, I commit myself to healthy eating.

Yours may look very different, and it will change from day to day. I also keep an eye on my bigger goals and vision and try to take at least one step toward those, even if it's small, every single day.

In summary

Identify what you're most passionate about right now. Get clear. Then get reasonable. Look at small, medium and big commitments you could make—and set your plan of action from there.

Conclusion and Next Steps

As I wrap up the writing of this book, I'm in Texas for the third time this year meeting with my friend and mentor Dr. Don Beck and his amazing team of "spiral wizards." I'm excited and optimistic for the future as more and more people become Agents for Change and begin to light the path forward to a new future while also making the world we're in better today.

I feel a tremendous amount of gratitude for the work of Clare W. Graves and Dr. Beck in uncovering the model for human change and development, as well as its practical application. Discovering this work has changed my life *completely*. I have gone from a person who was desperate to do something, but was overwhelmed by our polarized world, to being an Agent for Change with a powerful plan of action and brilliant set of tools to help me navigate. I feel like with The Change Code, I can actually be the change I want to see in the world.

At the beginning of this book, I shared The Change Code with you. I then shared how I've been applying this knowledge in my own life and efforts to make a difference, along with the specific tools that can help facilitate the process.

As I've been applying these tools with groups and individuals. I've been able to witness firsthand the key shifts that Colorado State University Professor Martin Carcasson promised. When we work together and collaborate, we can shift:

- **From wicked people to Wicked Problems:** We begin to realize that we're all in this together and we're doing the best we can. People with different viewpoints aren't evil and we are a lot more alike than we are different.

- **From adversaries to collaborators:** When we align our goals and take the time to understand and incorporate other viewpoints, we can work together. We don't have to be adversaries.

- **From facts as cherry-picked ammunition to facts as tools for addressing problems together:** When we begin to listen to and understand other perspectives, we find common ground. We begin to see that there are merits on both sides of a polarization. Learning to understand, map, and actively manage these polarizations brings people together.

- **From inciting the worst of human nature to bringing out the best of human nature:** We need to work to bring out the best of each other to tackle the challenges we face collectively. It all starts with just one person stepping forward and making the commitment to work to unite, rather than divide.[92]

My wish for you is that The Change Code allows you to better understand the shifts that are taking place on the planet right now. I hope this understanding will help reduce feelings of helplessness and fear of the unknown. I hope it gives meaning to what may seem like chaotic times, while also helping you feel empowered to fully step into who you're meant to be.

I have no doubt that you are a pathfinder and are here on this planet at this time for a reason. We need you now more than ever, and when you look deep inside yourself, you'll know that too.

"It's quite a burden lifted when we realize that we don't have to move the world, it's going to move anyway. This realization does not lessen our duty or our social obligation, it clarifies it."

~Ernest Holmes

My wish for the world is that love will prevail. I know that it will.

Together, let's create a new shared story for our turbulent times—and usher in a future in which we all collaborate, flourish and thrive.

Teach me what I cannot learn alone. Let us share what we know, and what we cannot fathom. Speak to me of mysteries, and let us never lie to one another. May our fierce and tender longing fuel the fire in our souls. When we stand side by side, let us dare to focus our desire on the truth. May we be reminders, each for the other, that the path of transformation passes through flames. To take one step is courageous: to stay on the path day after day, choosing the unknown, and facing yet another fear, that is nothing short of grace.

~Danna Faulds

And I'll leave you with one final quote:

Very few burdens are heavy if everyone lifts.

The Change Code Oath

I commit to being an Agent for Change.

I do my inner work first.

I encourage positive expression of every layer of the Change Code.

I find common ground and understand the group I am trying to help.

I build resilient community, connection and opportunities for communication.

I engage others in something bigger than all of us.

I develop new systems to solve more complex problems.

_____

Signature and Date

Find a downloadable, printable version at www.TheChangeCode.net/Resources.

Acknowledgments

It was early in 2019 when I discovered the work of Clare W. Graves. I had already committed myself to writing a book about making the world a better place. I was frustrated and exhausted by what I was seeing in the world and I knew we could do better. I sought to discover solutions for myself, as well as to share my findings with others.

I asked for guidance daily, and that guidance came in the form of a six-week class on Spiral Dynamics which was taught by Allan Watson at Unity of Portland. It changed everything for me, and I knew it was meant to be the underlying framework for my book.

I have deep gratitude for my mentors and teachers, both past and current. I'm especially grateful for Dr. Don Beck for creating multiple books and resources on Spiral Dynamics and for sharing his wisdom and friendship with me as I worked on this project and visited with him in Denton, Texas.

I'm also grateful to Steve McDonald and Nyck Jeanes in Byron Bay, Australia, for creating the Future Sense podcast and providing a modern context to Graves' theory and day-to-day events. I'm grateful for Two Foxes Singing (Nunpa) for sharing his story and Lakota wisdom, Dr. Barry Johnson for sharing his Polarity Mapping® process, E.J. Niles for her knowledge about Spiral Dynamics, incredible energy, and support, and to Michael Bernard Beckwith for changing my life with his Life Visioning process.

I also had the most amazing team, including my editor and book coach, Madeleine Eno from In the Write Place, my graphic designer, Jamie from Open Heart Designs, and my early reviewers and dear friends, Brandi Watts, Kami Norland, and Shannon Calhoun.

I owe many thanks to my wonderful and supportive husband and family, including our kids Kelsey, Em, Hannah, and Eliza, my granddaughter Payton—you are the future! Also, my parents, Eldon and Kathy, who helped me believe I can do anything, and Dave's inspiring parents, David and Connie, who have been wonderful cheerleaders during the long writing process.

I'm thankful to my four-legged assistants, Marley and Chewie, who made me get up from the computer from time to time to take a walk.

Finally, to my friends and colleagues in my Facebook Community, Agents for Change. Thank you for your kindness and support during the writing process. And of course, to Clare W. Graves and his Neverending Quest.

Appendix

Resources

Books:

Spiral Dynamics, Mastering Values, Leadership and Change by Don Edward Beck and Christopher Cowan

Spiral Dynamics in Action: Humanity's Master Code by Don Edward Beck, Teddy Hebo Larsen, Sergey Solonin, Dr. Rica Viljoen, Thomas Q. Johns

The Crucible: Forging South Africa's Future by Don Edward Beck, Graham Linscott

Clare W. Graves: His Life and His Work by Rainer Krumm, Benedikt Parstorfer

EMERGE!: The Rise of Functional Democracy and the Future of the Middle East by Elza Maalouf

Thinking in Systems by Donella H. Meadows

The Art of Extreme Self-Care: Transform Your Life One Month at a Time by Cheryl Richardson

The Second Mountain by David Brooks

The Abundant Community: Awakening the Power of Families and Neighborhoods by John McKnight and Peter Block

Polarity Management: Identifying and Managing Unsolvable Problems by Barry Johnson, Ph.D.

Life Visioning by Michael Bernard Beckwith

Media:

Buddify App for Meditation www.Buddify.com

HeartMath for Meditation www.HeartMath.com

Future Sense Podcast www.FutureSense.it

The Change Code Assessment www.TheChangeCode.net

The Change Code Resources www.TheChangeCode.net/Resources

Invictus (film)

Resources for Coming Together

The Agents for Change Facebook Group: A supportive group for leaders, visionaries, and changemakers to share ideas, inspiration, and best practices (www.facebook.com/groups/thechangecode)

ASK DEEP QUESTIONS: Jan Keck's mission is to create a world where everyone feels like they belong. Where strangers skip the small talk and connect meaningfully. Where relationships travel at the speed of vulnerability. And where we make each other feel heard, seen and valued. He created this amazing deck of conversation starter cards. Each deck of ASK DEEP QUESTIONS includes thoughtful questions that go below the surface to create meaningful connections. (www.jankeck.com/ask-deep-questions)

Jubilee: a media group that exists to create a movement of changemakers for human good. They create shareable human-centric videos that bridge people together, challenge controversial thinking, and inspire love. (www.youtube.com/user/jubileeproject)

The Common Party: a non-political, non-partisan social movement that is working to bring our country back together in these difficult and contentious times through the celebration of our overwhelming commonality. (www.thecommonparty.com)

Hidden Tribes: a year-long project to look at polarization, led by More in Common and launched in October 2019. (www.hiddentribe.us)

Make American Dinner Again: a group that facilitates dinners and positive discussions between individuals with a wide range of political beliefs. (www.makeamericadinneragain)

OpenMind: OpenMind is a psychology-based educational platform designed to depolarize campuses, companies, organizations, and communities. OpenMind helps people foster intellectual humility and mutual understanding, while equipping them with essential skills to engage constructively across differences. (www.openmindplatform.org)

Weave – The Social Fabric Project: A cultural movement to renew America's social fabric. Led by author and commentator – David Brooks – and The Aspen Institute. (www.aspensinstitute.com)

Ant Farm: A youth services and community-building non-profit in Sandy, Oregon. (www.antfarmyouthservices.com)

Make a Change Project: A free website with easy ways you can make a difference. (www.makeachangeproject.com)

Systems Innovation: An eLearning and collaborative platform for applying systems and complexity theory towards innovating new solutions to complex social, economic, technological and environmental challenges. (https://systemsinnovation.io)

Leadership & Organizational Styles

Worldview/ Layers	Description	Organizational Structure	Leadership Style	Maxim
Survival*Sense* **BEIGE**	Produces instinctive skills to survive in the rainforest, savanna, bush & tundra, as well as in cases of serious deprivation and tragedy.	Survival Band	**Nurturing Provider**	Satisfy basic needs
Tribal*Bond* **PURPLE**	Creates animistic thinking, bonds humans to closely-knit groups, and enriches inanimate objects with meaning and magical significance.	Tribal Order	**Traditional Protector**	Assure safety, uphold traditions
Impulse*Power* **RED**	Stimulates the impulsive self while generating powerful images of aggressiveness, conquest, and predator/ prey relationships.	Exploitive Empire	**Respected Boss**	Get respect, remain on top
Truth*Force* **BLUE**	Awakens transcendent purpose, impulse control; creates abstract causes, principles; focus on future reward; disciplined and dedicated.	Order-Driven Hierarchy	**Rightful Authority**	Follow the ordained rules
Strive*Drive* **ORANGE**	Forges the autonomous self, creates the algorithms of strategy, changeability and pragmatism; stresses status, winning and success.	Strategic Enterprise	**Win:Win**	Win the game, strive to be the best

Worldview/ Layers	Description	Organizational Structure	Leadership Style	Maxim
Human*Equity* **GREEN**	Rejects authoritarian and materialistic codes while exploring the inner self and inner selves of others. Searched for harmony, supports egalitarian communities in a quest for peace and caring.	Social Network	**Sensitive Facilitator**	Enable human potential, including mine
Holistic*Flow* **YELLOW**	Integral, systemic, natural works to restore human viability to a world convoluted by First Tier systems, both their successes and failures. Legitimizes all of the layers; works to keep each healthy and open to movement along the Spiral.	Competent Partner	**Systemic Navigator**	Do what I know is needed, with awareness of the impact on all life
Integral*Being* **TUR-QUOISE**	Detects holistic energy flows that bind everything together. Constructs large-scale mandates in acting on behalf of all life. Nurtures all human manifestations that contribute to "the whole," while sensing big picture perspectives and comprehensive initiatives.	Holistic Organism	**Global Catalyst**	Ensure that both humanity and planet thrive
CORAL	TBD	TBD	TBD	TBD

Source: Christopher Cooke at 5 Deep Limited www.5deep.org

Notes

1. Jason Daley, "Syndemic: The Little-Known Buzzword That Describes Our Troubled Times," Smithsonian.com, January 30, 2019, https://www.smithsonianmag.com/smart-news/syndemic-little-known-buzzword-describes-our-troubled-times-180971381/?fbclid=IwAR2i6HQ334XwvhuNe9wkcmu6djOLqbtetr7ORpFwCU3XzQRPT4rDVEpQqAc.

2. "Polarization," Oxford Learner's Dictionaries, accessed October 10, 2019, https://www.oxfordlearnersdictionaries.com/us/definition/english/polarization?fbclid=IwAR21wSIxyRjnwnuokLbNJEh9pp9Ly-WGk7lUCODPqhhpt35kZ8ePNxQ307gY.

3. Ashok Gangadean, *Awakening the Global Mind: A New Philosophy for Healing Ourselves and Our World* (Boulder: Sounds True, 2008).

4. "Wicked Problem," Wicked Problems, accessed October 10, 2019, https://www.wickedproblems.com/1_wicked_problems.php?fbclid=IwAR19GQxTD-h-A04EAHw16PZV9Nizu_3Ph_V_wsClCf-NuErMDWYEfI_bh2wQ.

5. "Wicked Problem"

6. Barry Johnson, "Polarity Management: Identifying and Managing Unsolvable Problems by Barry Johnson," Polarity Management™, accessed October 10, 2019, http://www.uuce.org/assets/McKandershHandout.pdf.

7. Martin Carcasson, "Introduction to Deliberative Engagement, Feb. 2018 (1 of 3)," YouTube, February 12, 2018, https://www.youtube.com/watch?v=hQDL7drhiL0&fbclid=IwAR22cwA2M1tyr-wNn-dEoLVBQWGtzqmiOrznSlFYC4mCQUt-jVN_KUTbkvbg.

8. Laura Paisley, "Political Polarization at Its Worst Since the Civil War," USC News, November 8, 2016, https://news.usc.edu/110124/political-polarization-at-its-worst-since-the-civil-war-2/?fbclid=IwAR1EiFsYRDseF-i2iLzq4ziuXA--XiUFTfWG9QkORalHCdn5s2rQ4F0OZJA.

9. Michael Barber and Nolan McCarty, "Causes and Consequences of Polarization," in Solutions to Political Polarization in America, ed. Nathaniel Persily (Cambridge: Cambridge University Press, 2015), 19-53.

10. HiddenTribes, "Hidden Tribes: A Study of America's Polarized Landscape" (More in Common, 2018), https://www.moreincommon.com/hidden-tribes.

11. Hidden Tribes, "The Hidden Tribes of America" (More in Common, 2018), https://hiddentribes.us/.

12. Barber and McCarty, "Causes and Consequences of Polarization."

13. Shankar Vedantam, "Nature, Nurture and Your Politics," npr, October 8, 2018, https://www.npr.org/templates/transcript/transcript.php?storyId=654127241&fbclid=IwAR0V4GSQwKLtn2ocV_QP-KNcVWbt0plI9cYVgwtYVzoJvyWNChLIX6uTCLvA.

14. Bertrand Russel, "The Triumph of Stupidity," in Mortals and Others: Bertrand Russell's American Essays, ed. H. Ruja, 2 vols. (New York: Routledge, 1933).

15. Associated Press, "Oregon Republican Senators End Walkout over Climate-Change Bill," NBC News, June 29, 2019, https://www.nbcnews.com/politics/politics-news/oregon-republican-senators-end-walkout-over-carbon-bill-n1024976?fbclid=IwAR1I7r_gPNxcMhie5o815X04KFxHpbMU-WYiiHsinBYwM5V8rqqmza2SkB_4.

16. Owen Daugherty, "GOP Oregon Lawmaker Who Threatened Police During Climate Bill Boycott Hit with Formal Complaint," The Hill, June 30, 2019.

17. Kyle Dropp and Brendan Nyhan, "One-Third Don't Know Obamacare and Affordable Care Act Are the Same," New York Times, February 7, 2017, https://www.nytimes.com/2017/02/07/upshot/one-third-dont-know-obamacare-and-affordable-care-act-are-the-same.html?fbclid=IwAR1NleRUw0D-KqdWdt1iWG2-5DL0kARiPDnpTGVvulThyfr7fA8pfQcBmhWw.

18. Jennifer L. McCoy, "Extreme Political Polarization Weakens Democracy – Can The US Avoid That Fate?," The Conversation, October 31, 2018, https://theconversation.com/extreme-political-polarization-weakens-democracy-can-the-us-avoid-that-fate-105540?fbclid=IwAR0L4CNWZYIXkO2q_vhWk2sXtlAkIRvz3Vf0NsbrnjMAkv91mTTgM83iYmE.

19. Cohn, "Polarization Is Dividing American Society, Not Just Politics"

20. Mike Gilbert, "Applying Spiral Dynamics to Our Lives – A Conversation with Don Beck," Conscious Bridge, January 1, 2016, http://consciousbridge.com/wordpress/media/conscious-bridge-radio/applying-spiral-dynamics-to-our-lives-a-conversation-with-don-beck/.

21. Noaimiloa, "The Amazing Spiral," Live Journal, July 26, 2006, https://noaimiloa.livejournal.com/15303.html.

22. Kelly Tatera, "Neuroscience Reveals the Differences Between Republican and Democrat Brains," The Science Explorer, 2016, February 1, 2016, http://thescienceexplorer.com/humanity/neuroscience-reveals-differences-between-republican-and-democrat-brains?fbclid=IwAR38mtWgoET-ItTHY-lQdN-QOBo-pc_ZYXuZ6_vc2sa-p5XfhDJRjPlnegUA.

23. Christopher C. Cowan and Don Edward Beck, Spiral Dynamics: Mastering Values, Leadership, and Change (New York: Blackwell, 1995), 30

24. Clare W. Graves, "Human Nature Prepares for a Momentous Leap," The Futurist, 1974, pp. 72-87.

25. Cowan and Beck, *Spiral Dynamics*.

26. Clare W. Graves, *The Never Ending Quest: Dr. Clare W. Graves Explores Human Nature: A Treatise on an emergent cyclica*, 2nd ed., ed. Christopher C. Cowan and Todorovic Natasha (Santa Barbara: ECLET, 2005), 399.

27. David Burkus, "Why Whole Foods Builds Its Entire Business on Teams," Forbes, June 8, 2016, https://www.forbes.com/sites/davidburkus/2016/06/08/why-whole-foods-build-their-entire-busi-ness-on-teams/?fbclid=IwAR0hUNUSgIIRGMkt-6oTk5VIOSjyD3EzcRn_k0uN-1ihGmzWjC-CEo3nMNE8#7d750b073fa1; John Mackey, "The Upward Flow of Human Development," Whole Foods Market, May 1, 2006, https://www.wholefoodsmarket.com/blog/john-mackeys-blog/upward-flow-hu-man%C2%A0development?fbclid=IwAR370xY7B-nD7ahDtdQ_nsCJzFbF9T42_rRBBYp__Ox_z3C4RSUgo3XWV1w.

28. Sarah Butler and Zoe Wood, "Amazon to Buy Whole Foods Market in $13.7bn Deal," *The Guardian*, June 16, 2017, https://www.theguardian.com/business/2017/jun/16/amazon-buy-whole-foods-market-organic-food-fresh

29. Steve McDonald, "ELEV8.live Switzerland 2018," Eman8, June 9, 2018, https://www.eman8.net

30. "About Us," Extinction Rebellion, accessed November 7, 2019, https://rebellion.earth/the-truth/about-us/

31. Graves, "Human Nature Prepares for a Momentous Leap"

32. Steve McDonald, "Future Sense " Apple Podcasts Preview, accessed October 11, 2019, https://podcasts.apple.com/au/podcast/future-sense/id1448122835

33. World Domination Summit, "WDS 2019 Main Stage Keynote - Nadya Okamoto on Period Poverty and the Potential of Generation Z," YouTube, 2019, https://www.youtube.com/watch?v=gytCx-9zntp0&fbclid=IwAR3nFtgmAhL5bfCmLwkB0xYriEK7Yxnid3BhNVQiYCGEXzipv4vle-mwJ2E.

34. Graves, "Human Nature Prepares for a Momentous Leap"

35. Ken Wilber, *Trump and A Post-Truth World* (Boulder: Shambhala, 2017), 8.

36. "Panentheism," Wikipedia, accessed October 11, 2019, https://en.wikipedia.org/wiki/Panentheism

37. Graves, *The Never Ending Quest*, 245.

38. "Third tier," Integral + Life, accessed October 11, 2019, https://integrallife.com/glossary/third-Ter/

39. "An Intro to Spiral Dynamics & The Tiers of Consciousness," Adam Siddiq, accessed Octo-ber 11, 2019, https://adamsiddiq.com/2017/08/062/?fbclid=IwAR1-4dBB70pV42ixx5zV9AAsQjDwM-WX6-n8Xf5vbYqssXS8p_NWpe6W1j6w.

40. Steve McDonald, "Altered States and Change," Eman8, accessed November 7, 2019, https://www.eman8.net/change/altered-states/

41. David Brooks, The Second Mountain: The Quest for a Moral Life (New York: Random House, 2019).

42. Rupert Sheldrake, Science and Spiritual Practices: Transformative Experiences and Their Effects on Our Bodies, Brains, and Health (Berkeley: Counterpoint, 2017).

43. Young Entrepreneur Council, "Why Sustainable Branding Matters," Forbes, August 20, 2018, https://www.forbes.com/sites/theyec/2018/08/20/why-sustainable-branding-matters/?fbclid=IwAR0h-q3gZrMbXt1n5dgQbeGO3D-hzfWueD6_yP8d1qroiGww9VNz20CeTK-c#654ec2935b6e.

44. Viviane Richter, "The Big Five Mass Extinctions," Cosmos - The science of everything, accessed October 11, 2019, https://cosmosmagazine.com/palaeontology/big-five-extinctions?fbclid=IwAR37wk-72dCmI_qMC_RuDi58gIvN1DPxE_wMT4_7zwrG3DD8U-y9wdJxc8-c.

45. "Microsoft AI TV Commercial, 'Saving Snow Leopards' Featuring Common," Ispot.tv, 2019, https://www.ispot.tv/ad/o_yG/microsoft-ai-saving-snow-leopards?fbclid=IwAR0T-1Jxqi14eOX-AbkK8bQits7YREHahafEV-LaFF8VUPWiqqgFReqr9D5s.

46. Grace Hauck, "Columbus Day: Celebrating Cultural Heritage, or the Colonization of Native Americans?" USA Today, October 12, 2019, https://www.usatoday.com/story/news/nation/2019/10/12/columbus-day-indigenous-peoples-day-why-some-change-name/3932258002/

47. "Current World Population," Worldometers, accessed October 11, 2019, https://www.worldometers.info/world-population/?fbclid=IwAR0-rVcV5KaR_QowEy5A6GXzmo8RmYEGXzIkb8ctzm-j5uQl2AvjP30rDK3c.

48. Donella H. Meadows and Diana Wright, Thinking in Systems: A Primer (White River Junction: Chelsea Green Pub, 2008).

49. Meadows and Wright, Thinking in Systems.

50. Anna Birney, Joshua Cubista and Laura Winn, Systems Change Education in an Innovation Context: Report & Reflections (2019), http://systemschangeeducation.com/wp-content/uploads/2019/04/Systems-Change-Education-Report-daniela_papi.pdf.

51. McDonald, "ELEV8.live Switzerland 2018".

52. McDonald, "ELEV8.live Switzerland 2018".

53. Michael Bernard Beckwith, Life Visioning: A Transformative Process for Activating Your Unique Gifts and Highest Potential (Boulder: Sounds True, 2013).

54. Kathleen McCoy, "How A State Court and A Tribal Court Collaborate on The Kenai," Alaska Public Media, July 11, 2018, https://www.alaskapublic.org/2018/07/11/how-a-state-court-and-a-tribal-court-collaborate-on-the-kenai/?fbclid=IwAR3-ur4Z4LLA15meH7-0h9x1AMHUCM5UJ8kbo8i-1eQ8woaFBBvVO8roJKm0.

55. World Economic Forum, "Finland's Education System Is One of The Best in The World - This Is How It Works," Facebook, accessed October 11, 2019, https://www.facebook.com/watch/?v=1216540928500160.

56. Newsroom, "Empathy? In Denmark They're Learning It in School," Morning Future, 2019, https://www.morningfuture.com/en/article/2019/04/26/empathy-happiness-school-denmark/601/?fbclid=IwAR3nHyclE4lcH9-M8z_23tUcx3sT6GgqMsGoEHpvQMOz56Ni_FfIpC0a8Aw.

57. United Nations, "World Happiness Report 2019" (2019), https://worldhappiness.report/?fbclid=IwAR3EjJarU0mkpSrMpmvSbaDssBnTrFVIB3q6-EYDl5YPos-hehMEuZQXHDY.

58. "Dr. Dweck's Research Into Growth Mindset Changed Education Forever," Mindset Works, accessed October 11, 2019, https://www.mindsetworks.com/science/?fbclid=IwAR1G-7j584DYS9-KH-CP9MfhLApONAIT1DznMqUQeoxEIKhgq7ZlgiA2UPvs.

59. Graves, The Never Ending Quest, 477-478.

60. Savannah Cox, "20 Powerful Quotes by Pope Francis on Climate Change and The Environment," All That's Interesting, June 18, 2015, https://allthatsinteresting.com/pope-francis-climate-change-quotes?fbclid=IwAR2_Na23n6wo2_AKQnWVy8E4T9h5Xa488O9PahVkGe6A8yEL2zibBfFFip4#13.

61. Gabby Bernstein, "Gabbybernstein: Stories," Instagram, accessed October 11, 2019, https://www.instagram.com/stories/highlights/17851252963502016/.

62. Douglas Broom, "How Three US Cities Are Using Data to End Homelessness," World Economic Forum, March 18, 2019, https://www.weforum.org/agenda/2019/03/united-states-cities-using-data-to-end-homelessness/?fbclid=IwAR3UuNSiITczyuokLhsai3WFq65OIbKJUpue1OcdfGAH06em6y6nOAtQEaQ.

63. Most seminars offered by Western organizations focus on Western Democracy, Governance and Empowerment of Women…". "Category Archives: Arab Women," Build Palestine Blog, accessed October 11, 2019, http://www.humanemergencemiddleeast.org/build-palestine-blog/category/arab-women?fbclid=IwAR2uUKmyC1oIOHQmCsOTNsFRTmQH9HN1fxyehASx9vLxIAYh9PjndxXK8zg.

64. Paul Schoemaker, "The 3 Decisions That Made Mandela a Great Leader," INC, December 5, 2013, https://www.inc.com/paul-schoemaker/what-made-nelson-mandela-such-a-great-leader.html?fbclid=IwAR1xiakitHkRZ1lm2mBo-QNwi94NFv-qo56hMF1WOmOenqLTtDhv3kIMQTs.

65. Saul McLeod, "Robbers Cave," Simply Psychology, 2008, https://www.simplypsychology.org/robbers-cave.html?fbclid=IwAR1R7JEsk6ZoPdzkH6xd-ckpKtlR-d6CgRKe3dQJUdIq1Sq-O8tAKt3vBoc.

66. "South Africa National Rugby Union Team," Wikipedia, accessed October 11, 2019, https://en.wikipedia.org/w/index.php?oldid=920575002.

67. "Cold War," Wikipedia, accessed October 10, 2019, https://en.wikipedia.org/wiki/Cold_War.

68. Tom Kertscher, "90% of Americans Back Background Checks for All Gun Sales?," Politifact Wisconsin, October 3, 2017, https://www.politifact.com/wisconsin/statements/2017/oct/03/chris-abele/do-90-americans-support-background-checks-all-gun-/?fbclid=IwAR32U6lhHBUA3e94PVOdns547POg8e3QOqPkpTN9aOWS6lLTK_ktcenMHH8.

69. "Jubilee Project," YouTube, https://www.youtube.com/user/jubileeProject/, accessed October 10, 2019.

70. Carlos Lozada, "Are We Telling The Right Story of America?," Washington Post, June 27, 2019, https://www.washingtonpost.com/outlook/2019/06/27/are-we-telling-right-story-america/?fbclid=IwAR0sjiIq4v2uBZOfO78kqgY6BLKjOqxLsZd6wM6Jt0J8Q2Dgdjj7SMselrI.

71. McCoy, "How A State Court and A Tribal Court Collaborate on The Kenai"; Jeremy Flood, "The Revolution Must Be Felt," Medium, December 3, 2016, https://medium.com/m/global-identity?redirectUrl=https%3A%2F%2Fextranewsfeed.com%2Fthe-revolution-must-be-felt-6e383217be89; Wilber, Trump and A Post-Truth World.

72. Steve Rathje, "The Power of Framing: It's Not What You Say, It's How You Say It," The Guardian, July 20, 2017, https://www.theguardian.com/science/head-quarters/2017/jul/20/the-power-of-framing-its-not-what-you-say-its-how-you-say-it?fbclid=IwAR0xlUxX4QIMI4mxlsyC-NSEQapAZkFnXURwbemWveK5DR_sXMMoy4ukKp0.

73. FORA.tv, "Idea Framing, Metaphors, and Your Brain - George Lakoff," YouTube, 2008, https://www.youtube.com/watch?v=S_CWBjyIERY&fbclid=IwAR2SUt9KAfIAEbj6Dh0LFuS-A8E8wC-cMV_NpBlzZPtN4cDpOeAc7rapigHc.

74. Ennuid, "George Lakoff's "Framing 101"," Medium, May 27, 2017, https://medium.com/@ennuid/george-lakoffs-framing-101-7b88e9c91dac.

75. TEDx Talks, "How Shopping Carts Will Transform Society," YouTube, May 20, 2015, https://www.youtube.com/watch?v=zPm70E8xbug&feature=youtu.be&fbclid=IwAR1J63b8kOYn6Z3Nk4w-JxrB0_PUr1LsrkyzHXvpPh7hzlgY1ZcL8H_nfwJs; Karen McNenny, "Community is The Cure," accessed October 11, 2019, http://www.karenmcnenny.com/?fbclid=IwAR109Z4bJjVNt45I6ezkJA_FsHiF-cEaA9T5zBsN_MHv1JWu39-q0kWEXjHA.

76. Brooks, The Second Mountain.

77. Health Catalyst, "Full Documentary - The Story of New Ulm A Population Health Transformation HD," YouTube, September 27, 2016, https://www.youtube.com/watch?v=-y4F8AfJxa4&fbclid=IwAR3wi8klUiQGFz_rc16EspYkLCdEziZhjRIWXRfr-Hoo22e-O7NHVcZrDxA.

78. Peter Tubbs, "Students Sell Groceries in a Nebraska Town," Iowa Public Television, May 10, 2019, http://www.iptv.org/mtom/story/33887/students-sell-groceries-nebraska-town?fbclid=IwAR0bIhLuS-Pml7ITcj4jahP83sFS2rIWTw4htHqeIFI0FgW4Mk5yzrz38mZQ.

79. John MacKnight and Peter Block, The Abundant Community – Awakening the Power of Families and Neighborhoods, (London: Berrett-Koehler Publishers, 2010).

80. Montana State University, "Montana Horizons Programs: Transforming Communities from Striving to Thriving" (2010), http://msucommunitydevelopment.org/paul/content/MT%20Horizons2010_final-1.pdf.

81. Johnson, "Polarity Management".

82. Natalie May, Daniel M. Becker and Richard M. Frankel, Appreciative Inquiry in Healthcare: Positive Questions to Bring out The Best (Brunswick: Crown, 2011).

83. Jennifer Garvey Berger and Keith Johnston, Simple Habits for Complex Times: Powerful Practices for Leaders (Stanford: Stanford Business Books, 2016).

84. Carcasson, "Introduction to Deliberative Engagement, Feb. 2018 (1 of 3)"

85. Martin Carcasson, "Tackling Wicked Problems Through Deliberative Engagement," Colorado State University Center for Public Deliberation, October 2013, https://cpd.colostate.edu/wp-content/uploads/sites/4/2014/01/tackling-wicked-problems-through-deliberative-engagement.pdf?fbclid=IwAR3vks0G3poE9wF6hRKw0q9N8hA0GTxehriUAZKxRGZ4EEbw6GR9g0NpbYw.

86. "Butterfly Effect," Wikipedia, September 27, 2019, accessed October 11, 2019, https://en.wikipedia.org/w/index.php?oldid=918279858.

87. "Butterfly Effect"

88. McDonald, "ELEV8.live Switzerland 2018".

89. John P. Flintoff, "How to Change The World: John Paul Flintoff at Tedxathens 2012," YouTube, February 14, 2013, https://www.youtube.com/watch?v=JH6FBwbqxUA&fbclid=IwAR1wxgoYC-3cEZ3TBxflH3hVDKgH2JjgGq-hFvwa5qPHnmy5GgpzuAEF-36E.

90. Flintoff, "How to Change The World: John Paul Flintoff at Tedxathens 2012"

91. Joshua Becker, "The One Sentence You Need Each Day to Set Your Intention," Becoming-minimalist, 2019, https://www.becomingminimalist.com/intention-setting/?fbclid=IwAR0qT-8F3yKrLlqY3P8eq75ibgqdKCAJ3n6XUeBFRsCeBh3SFnHz0mg9StKk.

92. Martin Carcasson, "Addressing the Leadership Challenge of Polarization and Groupishness," Colorado State University Center for Public Deliberation, 2019, https://watercenter.colostate.edu/wp-content/uploads/sites/33/2019/02/Addressing-the-Leadership-Challenge-of-Polarization-and-Groupishness-Carcasson.pdf.

Bibliography

Adam Siddiq. "An Intro to Spiral Dynamics & The Tiers of Consciousness." Accessed October 11, 2019. https://adamsiddiq.com/2017/08/062/?fbclid=IwAR1-4dBB70pV42ixx5zV9AAsQjDwMWX6-n8X-f5vbYqssXS8p_NWpe6W1j6w.

Ant Farm (website). Accessed October 10, 2019. www.antfarmyouthservices.com.

Associated Press. "Oregon Republican Senators End Walkout over Climate-Change Bill." NBC News, June 29, 2019. https://www.nbcnews.com/politics/politics-news/oregon-republican-senators-end-walk-out-over-carbon-bill-n1024976?fbclid=IwAR1I7r_gPNxcMhie5o815X04KFxHpbMUWYiiHsinBY-wM5V8rqqmza2SkB_4.

Barber, Michael, and Nolan McCarty. "Causes and Consequences of Polarization." In *Solutions to Political Polarization in America,* edited by Nathaniel Persily, 19-53. Cambridge: Cambridge University Press, 2015.

Becker, Joshua. "The One Sentence You Need Each Day to Set Your Intention." Becomingminimalist, 2019. https://www.becomingminimalist.com/intention-setting/?fbclid=IwAR0qT8F3yKrLlqY3P8eq75ib-gqdKCAJ3n6XUeBFRsCeBh3SFnHz0mg9StKk.

Beckwith, Michael Bernard. *Life Visioning: A Transformative Process for Activating Your Unique Gifts and Highest Potential.* Boulder: Sounds True, 2013.

Bernstein, Gabby. "Gabbybernstein: Stories." Instagram. Accessed October 11, 2019. https://www.insta-gram.com/stories/highlights/17851252963502016/.

Birney, Anna, Joshua Cubista, and Laura Winn. *Systems Change Education in an Innovation Context: Report & Reflections.* 2019. http://systemschangeeducation.com/wp-content/uploads/2019/04/Sys-tems-Change-Education-Report-daniela_papi.pdf.

Brooks, David. *The Second Mountain: The Quest for a Moral Life.* New York: Random House, 2019.

Broom, Douglas. "How Three US Cities Are Using Data to End Homelessness." World Economic Forum, March 18, 2019. https://www.weforum.org/agenda/2019/03/united-states-cities-using-da-ta-to-end-homelessness/?fbclid=IwAR3UuNSiITczyuokLhsai3WFq65OIbKJUpue1OcdfGAH06e-m6y6nOAtQEaQ.

Build Palestine Blog. "Category Archives: Arab Women." Accessed October 11, 2019. http://www.humanemergencemiddleeast.org/build-palestine-blog/category/arab-women?fbclid=IwAR2uUK-myC1oIOHQmCsOTNsFRTmQH9HN1fxyehASx9vLxIAYh9PjndxXK8zg.

Burkus, David. "Why Whole Foods Builds Its Entire Business on Teams." Forbes, June 8, 2016. https://www.forbes.com/sites/davidburkus/2016/06/08/why-whole-foods-build-their-entire-busi-ness-on-teams/?fbclid=IwAR0hUNUSgIIRGMkt-6oTk5VIOSjyD3EzcRn_k0uN-1ihGmzWjC-CEo3nMNE8#7d750b073fa1.

Carcasson, Martín. "Addressing the Leadership Challenge of Polarization and Groupishness." Colorado State University Center for Public Deliberation, 2019. https://watercenter.colostate.edu/wp-content/uploads/sites/33/2019/02/Addressing-the-Leadership-Challenge-of-Polarization-and-Groupishness-Carcasson.pdf.

Carcasson, Martin. "Introduction to Deliberative Engagement, Feb. 2018 (1 of 3)." YouTube, February 12, 2018. https://www.youtube.com/watch?v=hQDL7drhiL0&fbclid=IwAR22cwA2M1tyr-wNn-dEoLVBQWGtzqmiOrznSlFYC4mCQUt-jVN_KUTbkvbg.

Carcasson, Martín. "Tackling Wicked Problems Through Deliberative Engagement." Colorado State University Center for Public Deliberation, October 2013. https://cpd.colostate.edu/wp-content/uploads/sites/4/2014/01/tackling-wicked-problems-through-deliberative-engagement.pdf?fbclid=IwAR3vks0G3poE9wF6hRKw0q9N8hA0GTxehriUAZKxRGZ4EEbw6GR9g0NpbYw.

Cohn, Nate. "Polarization Is Dividing American Society, Not Just Politics." *New York Times*, June 12, 2014. https://www.nytimes.com/2014/06/12/upshot/polarization-is-dividing-american-society-not-just-politics.html?fbclid=IwAR3G0CVj_uRxAxIw5hgsKSJDq9WY8W1_lkBjV9Suy-wL1P_gL8P-WpuTsVE4.

Cowan, Christopher C., and Don Edward Beck. *Spiral Dynamics: Mastering Values, Leadership, and Change.* New York: Blackwell, 1995.

Cox, Savannah. "20 Powerful Quotes by Pope Francis on Climate Change and The Environment." All That's Interesting, June 18, 2015. https://allthatsinteresting.com/pope-francis-climate-change-quotes?fbclid=IwAR2_Na23n6wo2_AKQnWVy8E4T9h5Xa488O9PahVkGe6A8yEL2zibBfFFip4#13.

Daley, Jason. "Syndemic: The Little-Known Buzzword That Describes Our Troubled Times." Smithsonian.com, January 30, 2019. https://www.smithsonianmag.com/smart-news/syndemic-little-known-buzzword-describes-our-troubled-times-180971381/?fbclid=IwAR2i6HQ334X-wvhuNe9wkcmu6djOLqbtetr7ORpFwCU3XzQRPT4rDVEpQqAc.

Daugherty, Owen. "GOP Oregon Lawmaker Who Threatened Police During Climate Bill Boycott Hit with Formal Complaint." *The Hill*, June 30, 2019.

Dropp, Kyle, and Brendan Nyhan. "One-Third Don't Know Obamacare and Affordable Care Act Are the Same." *New York Times*, February 7, 2017. https://www.nytimes.com/2017/02/07/upshot/one-third-dont-know-obamacare-and-affordable-care-act-are-the-same.html?fbclid=IwAR1NleRUw0D-KqdWdt1iWG2-5DL0kARiPDnpTGVvulThyfr7fA8pfQcBmhWw.

Ennuid. "George Lakoff's "Framing 101"" Medium, May 27, 2017. https://medium.com/@ennuid/george-lakoffs-framing-101-7b88e9c91dac.

Extinction Rebellion. "About Us." Extinction Rebellion. Accessed November 7, 2019, https://rebellion.earth/the-truth/about-us/

Flintoff, John Paul. "How to Change the World: John Paul Flintoff at Tedxathens 2012." YouTube, February 14, 2013. https://www.youtube.com/watch?v=JH6FBwbqxUA&fbclid=IwAR1wxgoYC-3cEZ3TBxflH3hVDKgH2JjgGq-hFvwa5qPHnmy5GgpzuAEF-36E.

Flood, Jeremy. "The Revolution Must Be Felt." Medium, December 3, 2016. https://medium.com/m/global-identity?redirectUrl=https%3A%2F%2Fextranewsfeed.com%2Fthe-revolution-must-be-felt-6e383217be89.

FORA.tv. "Idea Framing, Metaphors, and Your Brain - George Lakoff." YouTube, 2008. https://www.youtube.com/watch?v=S_CWBjyIERY&fbclid=IwAR2SUt9KAfIAEbj6Dh0LFuS-A8E8wC-cMV_NpBlzZPtN4cDpOeAc7rapigHc.

Future Sense Podcast (website). Accessed October 10, 2019. www.FutureSense.it.

Gangadean, Ashok. *Awakening the Global Mind: A New Philosophy for Healing Ourselves and Our World.* Boulder: Sounds True, 2008.

Garvey Berger, Jennifer, and Keith Johnston. *Simple Habits for Complex Times: Powerful Practices for Leaders.* Stanford: Stanford Business Books, 2016.

Gilbert, Mike. "Applying Spiral Dynamics to Our Lives – A Conversation with Don Beck." Concious Bridge, January 1, 2016. http://consciousbridge.com/wordpress/media/conscious-bridge-radio/applying-spiral-dynamics-to-our-lives-a-conversation-with-don-beck/.

Graves, Clare W. "Human Nature Prepares for a Momentous Leap." *The Futurist,* 1974, pp. 72-87.

Graves, Clare W. *The Never Ending Quest: Dr. Clare W. Graves Explores Human Nature: A Treatise on an emergent cyclica.* 2nd ed. Edited by Christopher C. Cowan and Todorovic Natasha. Santa Barbara: ECLET, 2005.

Hauck, Grace. "Columbus Day: Celebrating Cultural Heritage, or the Colonization of Native Americans?" USA Today, October 12, 2019. https://www.usatoday.com/story/news/nation/2019/10/12/columbus-day-indigenous-peoples-day-why-some-change-name/3932258002/

Health Catalyst. "Full Documentary - The Story of New Ulm A Population Health Transformation HD." YouTube, September 27, 2016. https://www.youtube.com/watch?v=-y4F8AfJxa4&fbclid=I-wAR3wi8klUiQGFz_rc16EspYkLCdEziZhjRIWXRfr-Hoo22e-O7NHVcZrDxA.

HeartMath for Meditation (website). Accessed October 10, 2019. www.HeartMath.com.

Hidden Tribes (website). Accessed October 10, 2019. www.HiddenTribes.us.

Hidden Tribes. "The Hidden Tribes of America." More in Common, 2018. https://hiddentribes.us/.

HiddenTribes. "Hidden Tribes: A Study of America's Polarized Landscape." More in Common, 2018. https://www.moreincommon.com/hidden-tribes.

Integral + Life. "Third Ter." Accessed October 11, 2019, https://integrallife.com/glossary/third-Ter/

Ispot.tv. "Microsoft AI TV Commercial, 'Saving Snow Leopards' Featuring Common." 2019. https://www.ispot.tv/ad/o_yG/microsoft-ai-saving-snow-leopards?fbclid=IwAR0T-1Jxqi14eOXAbkK8bQit-s7YREHahafEV-LaFF8VUPWiqqgFReqr9D5s.

Johnson, Barry. "Polarity Management: Identifying and Managing Unsolvable Problems by Barry Johnson." Polarity Management™. Accessed October 10, 2019. http://www.uuce.org/assets/McKandersHandout.pdf.

Kertscher, Tom. "90% of Americans Back Background Checks for All Gun Sales?" Politifact Wisconsin, October 3, 2017. https://www.politifact.com/wisconsin/statements/2017/oct/03/

chris-abele/do-90-americans-support-background-checks-all-gun-/?fbclid=IwAR32U6lhH-BUA3e94PVOdns547POg8e3Q0qPkpTN9aOWS6lLTK_ktcenMHH8.

Lozada, Carlos. "Are We Telling the Right Story of America?" *Washington Post*, June 27, 2019. https://www.washingtonpost.com/outlook/2019/06/27/are-we-telling-right-story-america/?fbclid=IwAR0s-jiIq4v2uBZOfO78kqgY6BLKjOqxLsZd6wM6Jt0J8Q2Dgdjj7SMselrI.

Mackey, John. "The Upward Flow of Human Development." Whole Foods Market, May 1, 2006. https://www.wholefoodsmarket.com/blog/john-mackeys-blog/upward-flow-human%C2%A0development?f-bclid=IwAR370xY7B-nD7ahDtdQ_nsCJzFbF9T42_rRBBYp__Ox_z3C4RSUgo3XWV1w.

MacKnight, John, and Block, Peter. *The Abundant Community – Awakening the Power of Families and Neighborhoods*. London: Berrett-Koehler Publishers, 2010.

Make American Dinner Again (website). Accessed October 10, 2019. www.MakeAmericaDinnerAgain.com.

May, Natalie, Daniel M. Becker, and Richard M. Frankel. *Appreciative Inquiry in Healthcare: Positive Questions to Bring out The Best*. Brunswick: Crown, 2011.

McCoy, Jennifer Lynn. "Extreme Political Polarization Weakens Democracy – Can The US Avoid That Fate?" The Conversation, October 31, 2018. https://theconversation.com/extreme-political-po-larization-weakens-democracy-can-the-us-avoid-that-fate-105540?fbclid=IwAR0L4CNWZYIX-kO2q_vhWk2sXtlAkIRvz3Vf0NsbrnjMAkv91mTTgM83iYmE.

McCoy, Kathleen. "How A State Court and A Tribal Court Collaborate on The Kenai." Alaska Public Media, July 11, 2018. https://www.alaskapublic.org/2018/07/11/how-a-state-court-and-a-trib-al-court-collaborate-on-the-kenai/?fbclid=IwAR3-ur4Z4LLA15meH7-0h9x1AMHUCM5UJ8k-bo8i1eQ8woaFBBvVO8roJKm0.

McDonald, Steve. "Altered States and Change." Eman8. Accessed November 7, 2019, https://www.eman8.net/change/altered-states/

McDonald, Steve. "ELEV8.live Switzerland 2018." Eman8, June 9, 2018. https://www.eman8.net

McDonald, Steve. "Future Sense." Apple Podcasts Preview. Accessed October 11, 2019, https://podcasts.apple.com/au/podcast/future-sense/id1448122835

McLeod, Saul. "Robbers Cave." Simply Psychology, 2008. https://www.simplypsychology.org/rob-bers-cave.html?fbclid=IwAR1R7JEsk6ZoPdzkH6xd-ckpKtlR-d6CgRKe3dQJUdIq1Sq-O8tAKt-3vBoc.

McNenny, Karen. "Community is The Cure." Accessed October 11, 2019. http://www.karenmcnenny.com/?fbclid=IwAR109Z4bJjVNt45I6ezkJA_FsHiFcEaA9T5zBsN_MHv1JWu39-q0kWEXjHA.

Meadows, Donella H., and Diana Wright. *Thinking in Systems: A Primer*. White River Junction: Chelsea Green Pub, 2008.

Mindset Works. "Dr. Dweck's Research into Growth Mindset Changed Education Forever." Accessed October 11, 2019. https://www.mindsetworks.com/science/?fbclid=IwAR1G-7j584DYS9-KHCP9M-fhLApONAIT1DznMqUQeoxEIKhgq7ZlgiA2UPvs.

Montana State University. "Montana Horizons Programs: Transforming Communities from Striving to Thriving." 2010. http://msucommunitydevelopment.org/paul/content/MT%20Horizons2010_final-1.pdf.

Newsroom. "Empathy? In Denmark They're Learning It in School." Morning Future, 2019. https://www.morningfuture.com/en/article/2019/04/26/empathy-happiness-school-denmark/601/?fbclid=I-wAR3nHyclE4lcH9-M8z_23tUcx3sT6GgqMsGoEHpvQMOz56Ni_FfIpC0a8Aw.

Noaimiloa. "The Amazing Spiral." Live Journal, July 26, 2006. https://noaimiloa.livejournal.com/15303.html.

OpenMind (website). Accessed October 10, 2019. https://openmindplatform.org/.

Oxford Learner's Dictionaries. "Polarization." Accessed October 10, 2019. https://www.oxfordlearners-dictionaries.com/us/definition/english/polarization?fbclid=IwAR21wSIxyRjnwnuokLbNJEh9pp9Ly-WGk7lUCODPqhhpt35kZ8ePNxQ307gY.

Paisley, Laura. "Political Polarization at Its Worst Since the Civil War." USC News, November 8, 2016. https://news.usc.edu/110124/political-polarization-at-its-worst-since-the-civil-war-2/?fbclid=IwA-R1EiFsYRDseF-i2iLzq4ziuXA--XiUFTfWG9QkORalHCdn5s2rQ4F0OZJA.

Rathje, Steve. "The Power of Framing: It's Not What You Say, It's How You Say It." *The Guardian*, July 20, 2017. https://www.theguardian.com/science/head-quarters/2017/jul/20/the-power-of-framing-its-not-what-you-say-its-how-you-say-it?fbclid=IwAR0xlUxX4QIMI4mxlsyC-NSEQapAZkFnXUR-wbemWveK5DR_sXMMoy4ukKp0.

Richter, Viviane. "The Big Five Mass Extinctions." Cosmos - The Science of Everything. Accessed October 11, 2019. https://cosmosmagazine.com/palaeontology/big-five-extinctions?fbclid=IwAR-37wk72dCmI_qMC_RuDi58gIvN1DPxE_wMT4_7zwrG3DD8U-y9wdJxc8-c.

Russel, Bertrand. "The Triumph of Stupidity." In *Mortals and Others: Bertrand Russell's American Essays*. Edited by H. Ruja. 2 vols., 27–28. New York: Routledge, 1933.

Sarah, Butler and Wood, Zoe. "Amazon to Buy Whole Foods Market in $13.7bn Deal." *The Guardian*, June 16, 2017. https://www.theguardian.com/business/2017/jun/16/amazon-buy-whole-foods-market-organic-food-fresh

Schoemaker, Paul. "The 3 Decisions That Made Mandela a Great Leader." *INC*, December 5, 2013. https://www.inc.com/paul-schoemaker/what-made-nelson-mandela-such-a-great-leader.html?fb-clid=IwAR1xiakitHkRZ1lm2mBo-QNwi94NFv-qo56hMF1WOmOenqLTtDhv3kIMQTs.

Sheldrake, Rupert. *Science and Spiritual Practices: Transformative Experiences and Their Effects on Our Bodies, Brains, and Health*. Berkeley: Counterpoint, 2017.

St. John of the Cross. "ST. John of the Cross, 16th Century: The Dark Night of the Soul." Makeheaven.com, July 9, 2019. http://makeheaven.com/st-john-of-the-cross.html?fbclid=IwAR2LS2F0ezuR5X-q5q-3ZXEzzJ1v1jQnTxodYSMlwj0fJIuDhyiLj-3SNOYk.

Tatera, Kelly. "Neuroscience Reveals the Differences Between Republican and Democrat Brains." The Science Explorer, 2016, February 1, 2016. http://thescienceexplorer.com/humanity/neuroscience-re-veals-differences-between-republican-and-democrat-brains?fbclid=IwAR38mtWgoET-ItTHY-lQd-NQOBo-pc_ZYXuZ6_vc2sa-p5XfhDJRjPlnegUA.

TEDx Talks. "How Shopping Carts Will Transform Society." YouTube, May 20, 2015. https://www. youtube.com/watch?v=zPm70E8xbug&feature=youtu.be&fbclid=IwAR1J63b8kOYn6Z3Nk4w-JxrB0_PUr1LsrkyzHXvpPh7hzlgYlZcL8H_nfwJs.

The Aspen Institute. "Weave – The Social Fabric Project." The Aspen Institute. Accessed October 10, 2019. https://www.aspeninstitute.org/programs/weave-the-social-fabric-initiative/.

The Common Party (website). Accessed October 10, 2019. www.TheCommonParty.com.

The Devine Life Society. "Sivananda Daily Reading." Accessed October 11, 2019, http://sivanandaonline. org/public_html/

The Flip Side (website). Accessed October 10, 2019. https://www.theflipside.io.

Tubbs, Peter. "Students Sell Groceries in a Nebraska Town." Iowa Public Television, May 10, 2019. http://www.iptv.org/mtom/story/33887/students-sell-groceries-nebraska-town?fbclid=IwAR0bI-hLuSPml7ITcj4jahP83sFS2rIWTw4htHqeIFI0FgW4Mk5yzrz38mZQ.

United Nations. "World Happiness Report 2019." 2019. https://worldhappiness.report/?fbclid=I-wAR3EjJarU0mkpSrMpmvSbaDssBnTrFVIB3q6-EYDl5YPos-hehMEuZQXHDY.

Vedantam, Shankar. "Nature, Nurture and Your Politics." npr, October 8, 2018. https://www.npr. org/templates/transcript/transcript.php?storyId=654127241&fbclid=IwAR0V4GSQwKLtn2ocV_QPKNcVWbt0plI9cYVgwtYVzoJvyWNChLIX6uTCLvA.

Wicked Problems. "Wicked Problem." Accessed October 10, 2019. https://www.wickedproblems. com/1_wicked_problems.php?fbclid=IwAR19GQxTD-h-A04EAHw16PZV9Nizu_3Ph_V_wsCl-CfNuErMDWYEfI_bh2wQ.

Wikipedia. "Butterfly Effect." Accessed October 11, 2019, September 27, 2019. https://en.wikipedia.org/w/index.php?oldid=918279858.

Wikipedia. "Cold War." Accessed October 10, 2019. https://en.wikipedia.org/wiki/Cold_War.

Wikipedia. "Panentheism." Accessed October 11, 2019. https://en.wikipedia.org/wiki/Panentheism

Wikipedia. "South Africa National Rugby Union Team." Accessed October 11, 2019. https://en.wikipedia. org/w/index.php?oldid=920575002.

Wilber, Ken. *Trump and A Post-Truth World*. Boulder: Shambhala, 2017.

World Domination Summit. "WDS 2019 Main Stage Keynote - Nadya Okamoto on Period Poverty and the Potential of Generation Z." YouTube, 2019. https://www.youtube.com/watch?v=gytCx9zntp0&f-bclid=IwAR3nFtgmAhL5bfCmLwkB0xYriEK7Yxnid3BhNVQiYCGEXzipv4vle-mwJ2E.

World Economic Forum. "Finland's Education System Is One of The Best in The World - This Is How It Works." Facebook. Accessed October 11, 2019. https://www.facebook.com/watch/?v=1216540928500160.

Worldometers. "Current World Population." Accessed October 11, 2019. https://www.worldometers.info/world-population/?fbclid=IwAR0-rVcV5KaR_QowEy5A6GXzmo8RmYEGXzIkb8ctzmj5uQl2Av-jP30rDK3c.

Young Entrepreneur Council. "Why Sustainable Branding Matters." Forbes, August 20, 2018. https://www.forbes.com/sites/theyec/2018/08/20/why-sustainable-branding-matters/?fbclid=IwAR0hq3gZ-rMbXt1n5dgQbeGO3D-hzfWueD6_yP8d1qroiGww9VNz20CeTK-c#654ec2935b6e.

YouTube. "Jubilee Project." Accessed October 10, 2019, https://www.youtube.com/user/jubileeProject/.

About the Author

Monica Bourgeau is an entrepreneur, coach, consultant, speaker, and healthcare executive who studies and leads personal and organizational change. For the past two decades, she has led healthcare transformation initiatives across the U.S. with a focus on rural health. She has been the Executive Director & COO for national healthcare non-profits, and has also worked for a health insurance company/third party administrator (TPA). She led the nation's first Rural Medicine Hackathon and Hacking Medicaid events with teams from MIT's Hacking Medicine Program.

Monica is a member of several non-profit boards. She's also a frequent guest speaker on the topics of change leadership and business transformation. She has a bachelor's degree in Psychology from Colorado State University, a Master's degree in Management with an emphasis on Organizational Leadership from Warner Pacific University, and has completed an MBA Foundations program from the University of Montana.

Her work has been featured on The Huffington Post, Elephant Journal, Medium, Startup Nation, and in *Along These Lines*, a college writing textbook.

Monica believes we each have a duty to help leave the world a little better than we found it. She is passionate about innovation, leadership, spirituality, animals and animal rescue, and the environment, and is a member of the Portland chapter of Conscious Capitalism.

Monica grew up in rural Western Montana and still visits there often. She lives with her family and their two rescue dogs in beautiful Portland, Oregon.

For more information, visit www.MonicaBourgeau.com

www.ingramcontent.com/pod-product-compliance
Lightning Source LLC
Chambersburg PA
CBHW030243030426
42336CB00009B/237